A Tree Grows in Thai Nguyen

Sarge

A Tree Grows in Thai Nguyen

Sarge

Copyright © 2017 by Bill McDonald

ISBN: 978-1-61529-185-4

Vision Publishing
P.O. Box 1680
Ramona, CA 92065
1 (760) 789-4700
www.booksbyvision.org

Acknowledgements

Acknowledging and giving credit where credit is due...

In one place, it says that with God all things are possible; THIS would not have happened without God.

There is no way this would work without Mrs. Susan M. McDonald period!

Both of us cherish the financial support, intercession support, the logistical support, the encouragement support, the care package support, the personal visit support, and all other forms of support we enjoy from LOTS of people.

No token line here, we ALL are part of what the Father is doing through ALL of us here in northern Vietnam.

Table of Contents

Introduction 5

Chapter 1 How did that happen? 7

Chapter 2 Things in Common 13

Chapter 3 What Were We Thinking 17

Chapter 4 Some Amazing Stuff 25

Chapter 5 Measurements 39

Chapter 6 For the Duration 43

Chapter 7 Confirmation 53

Chapter 8 Cost 63

Chapter 9 Expectations 69

Chapter 10 Playing Hurt 77

Chapter 11 Fruit that Will Remain 83

Chapter 12 Imagination or Vision 95

Conclusion 103

Epilogue 105

Introduction

Visiting Vietnam – we just happened to be in the neighborhood
Sarge – Bill McDonald

Neither one of us wanted to be in Vietnam, we thought that we'd
be in Honduras by now, sipping piña coladas (alcohol free, of
course), and doing "m" work. "M" work is a piece of cake in
Honduras.

Just recently, we became the first foreigners ever to be given a
teaching contract with a state university, a work permit, and visas
on an individual basis. This bears repeating: In late March 2014,
Bill and Sue were given a teaching contract – through June 2015, a
work permit valid until March 2017, and visas that are good for a
year and allow us to travel in and out of Vietnam as often as we
need or want to; AND, this was the first time EVER that this has
occurred, in Thai Nguyen University and in Thai Nguyen, Vietnam
at a minimum and possibly in all of Vietnam.

We are "on mission" in Vietnam. A retired American infantry
soldier turned university lecturer and his wife, a "retired"
American infantry soldier's family member – spouse turned "non-
teaching spouse" and teaching assistant/very occasional university
lecturer.

Since late August 2006, we just happened to be in the
neighborhood and, our mission is to be Visiting Vietnam until June
2021. We can "hear" Father saying, "[I] will visit you (Gen 50:24,
NKJV) *Vietnam*" (italic text added by author). Sometimes, we end
up somewhere we never would have expected.

Cảm ơn Chúa,
Bill & Sue McDonald

Chapter 1

How did that happen?

"All things work [out] for good for those who love G and to those who are called [by Him] (NKJV)."

"I couldn't have done this on a bet."

We were nearly broke. That is the truth and initially the reason I stopped at Evangel University, in Springfield Missouri, was because I needed some money. Several years earlier I had stopped there when it was still Evangel College; back when they did not accept "government money" (or maybe it was that they weren't eligible to receive federal monies). In the late 90's I'd been retired for a while, "trusting God," and stopped at EU "on a hunch." I needed the money that I would receive from the G.I. Bill; it was a very considerable sum. When the question was given to the person, "Do you take money from the G.I. Bill?" the person responded: "Sure, we take money from anywhere."

I wanted to "study" guitar and photography, anything that fulfilled the requirements to get the "free" cash! The person I met with began to talk about a "career path." I needed money, not another career! Before I knew it, I was a sophomore (almost) student at Evangel University and on my way to becoming a psychologist! And, the money from the G.I. Bill was GREAT; what a country!

Well, I will skip the whole first day of school – traditional student stuff and go straight to abnormal psychology. The diagnostic manual for psychologists is a VERY thick book and expensive. Basically, the book describes what "abnormal" is in precise measure. This day our class came across "post-traumatic stress disorder." Another student asked the professor what PTSD was and the professor responded something like, "Oh, it's something from the Vietnam War, sort of like shell shock back in World War II: but, I think a woman who has been raped experiences more trauma than a soldier did in Vietnam."

When I went back to university, I was nearly 50 years old, older than all the other students and most of the professors, too. Typically, I did not do much talking in class. But, this was different. After being called on I said: "Ma'am, with all due respect to a woman whose been a rape victim, there is no way that being raped one time equals the stress on a soldier who spent most of 12 – 13 months in combat in Vietnam." Then and there I decided I was going to prove her wrong.

Eventually, I was on a jet, headed to Ho Chi Minh City (Saigon in the war days) intending to locate and interview combat veterans from North Vietnam, South Vietnam, and American combat veterans who were on the same humanitarian trip I was on. The object was, go there and gather the data, return, report, and prove the "young whippersnapper professor" wrong. It didn't happen. That was July 2002. I've returned to Vietnam every year since that first trip, and we've been living and serving here since August 2006.

Most Americans are unaware that Ho Chi Minh, Vietnam's first president, respected and intended to be friendly to the United States of America. On September 2nd, 1945, surrounded by several American agents, Uncle Ho started his speech: "We believe that all people are created equal and are endowed by their Creator with certain unalienable rights. Among these are life, liberty and the pursuit of happiness." And then the second line: "Of course, that is a quote from the Declaration of Independence of that great nation, the United States of America." On March 8th, 1965 members of the United States Marines landed in an assault on "Red Beach" in Da Nang, (South) Vietnam, just a bit shy of exactly 20 years later.

About Me

I grew up in the Bronx, N.Y. I thank God, I did and I feel sorry for anyone who didn't. One of the things that we did there (and probably kids everywhere) was call out "DO OVER" when we needed another swing, another shot, another try at something. Sue and I call what we're doing in Vietnam a "DO OVER." Vietnam has been one united country since April 1975. And, without going near the "hot-button issues," we consider that we have been given a gigantic "DO OVER." Instead of stickball or scully, we've got a DO OVER in life. Being part of bringing life and that more abundantly to a group of people who desperately need a more abundant life is what we're about.

After achieving my Bachelor of Science in Psychology with a minor in Sociology, and then a Master of Social Work Degree, we now know that all of that was part of equipping us to serve in Vietnam. One of us is an in-class university lecturer and the other a non-teaching spouse (allowable only because of the Master's degree). Bill's first and subsequent trips to Vietnam with *Vet's With A Mission*, our becoming very, very good friends with seven Vietnamese women in the Da Nang area over a period of several years, and then getting involved with an organization sending English language lecturers to Vietnam, specifically to Thai Nguyen a very small city about 50 miles north of Hanoi, all contributed to our being where we are right now.

In late March 2014, we were given a teaching contract – through June 2015. In June 2015, we were waiting for our new visas, good for one year; INSTEAD, we were given resident cards, no visas required; AND, this was the first time EVER that this has occurred, in Thai Nguyen University or in Thai Nguyen at a minimum and possibly in all of Vietnam. How did this happen? Frankly, it has not been easy. It has been and is extremely costly in many ways. But, it is worth it.

In Review

Being alive during the whole thing we call "the War in Vietnam," being a "Vietnam-Era Veteran" (meaning one who did not participate in combat operations in that war), going 'back-to-school' (university), and ending up with two Master's degrees seems like a lot. Add to that working with an approved like-minded organization that sent us to Vietnam, initially for two years that turned into six, before returning "on our own." Back in Vietnam, we discovered that no one had ever done returning "on our own" successfully and no one in government or in our university knew how to make that happen; but, after we and several administrators knocked on some doors and made phone calls…just before Spring 2014… it happened! Amazing!

Think it Over

One of the best prayers I've ever heard was spoken to a man years ago by a parishioner who he was greeting at the end of a gathering. The parishioner said: "I pray that you will fulfill the purpose for which you were created." It is my favorite prayer and has become a personal goal, to help people find and fulfill the purpose for which they are created. I know that a truly abundant life can only come when one's purpose is being fulfilled.

1. Have you ever thought about the purpose for which you were created?

2. What was it that Father had in mind when you were formed in your mother's womb?

3. How far off-base, or how right-on-target has all the effort been so far?

4. What might everything and anything that you have done (or not) up until this point in life indicate what that "purpose for which you were created" might be?

5. How did you happen to get where you are right now; is it the place that was intended to be; is it the place where you belong?

My hope is that as you read further, and share in the adventure of our life, you will also find your greatest purpose, and determine to live it fully!!

Chapter 2

Things in Common

"Now all who believed were together, and had all things in common Acts 2:44 (NKJV)."

It has been said that December 31st, 2010 marked the end of the first decade ever that the country, Vietnam, did not have combat within its borders. The ancestors of present-day Vietnamese, practically all of them, knew war in one form or fashion or another. Of course, the United States of America shares the dubious distinction of having been one of the aggressors perpetuating some of that combat; quite a bit of it, as a matter of fact.

People living in Vietnam have fought against Portuguese, Chinese, French, Americans, and Cambodians. Vietnamese have fought with some of the allies of their aggressors. Entering a conversation about a "war in Vietnam" would beg the questions, "which one;" and, "which time?" Most of the Vietnamese people living in Vietnam today are younger the 30 years old; they do not know much about any of that war. And, like young people in many places, "ancient" history is not on the front burner of conversation. When brought face-to-face with the commonalities shared between Socialist Republic of Vietnam and the United States of America, most express disbelief, some express denial, many are surprised to shocked...I am referring to Americans who learn of this, mainly, and some Vietnamese too.

Vietnam was colonized; the United States was a colony. Vietnam fought a war to free itself from the control of a larger European country's control and government; the United States fought a war to gain independence from a larger European Empire. The American Revolution is looked upon by many Americans as an honorable endeavor, one that should be and is celebrated profusely every July 4th on Independence Day. The Vietnamese declared independence on September 2nd, 1945. Its first president quoted the American Declaration of Independence, referring to "that great nation, the United States of America." The Vietnamese fought against and defeated the French imperialists. Vietnam also experienced a civil war, North versus South; the Republic against a Confederacy. The United States experienced a civil war of its own; also, North against a renegade South, a Union pitted against its own countrymen who joined the Confederacy. Many Americans died at the hands of Americans; many Vietnamese died at the hands of Vietnamese. In the United States, the North "won;" and, in Vietnam the North also "won." After the American Civil War, poverty was common. In Vietnam, after their civil war, many people were poor too.

We have a lot in common.

Many Americans go into a building, kneel, and light a candle. He, or she, might say something like: "And Dad, if you've got the time, could you…?" Some ask something like, "put in a good word for me," or, "I need a sign from you," or something similar. Many Vietnamese light candles "for" their ancestors. Some have habits that amount to giving something to gain favor; or, some things are meant to provide for the comfort of an ancestor's spirit.

We have a lot in common.

Typically, Americans work from the age of about 18 until 65 years or so. Then, many Americans retire; live on a fixed income that has, hopefully, been 'fixed' well. What happens next often depends on how much money has been socked away. Many Vietnamese work until he is about 65 years old, or she is 55 years old. Then after retirement they live on a fixed income that is, frankly, microscopic when compared to the social security income of many Americans; unless a person has amassed a small fortune in one way or another. Life can be tough after retirement age.

We have a lot in common.

People in Vietnam cut each other off when driving; a bigger vehicle always has the "right-of-way." People in America throw trash out of car window and sometimes just after passing a sign that says that littering can result in a fine. Vietnamese people get impatient waiting in line and often step in front of anyone who has more to buy, just because they're in a hurry and are buying less. American people get huffed if the line at the fast food drive thru is not moving fast enough. American students at the university level have been known to take incredible measures to pass an exam, even when they have no idea about the subject on which the examination is being given. There are cameras watching every move anyone makes in test centers for standardized testing everywhere. Vietnamese university students just "work together" or send text messages.

We really do have a lot in common.

The longer I am in Vietnam the more things seem to be similar to or practically identical to things in the United States. The popular T-shirt slogan left over from the war states it succinctly, "same, same but different."

People here in Vietnam do all sorts of things to appease spirits, gain favor with gods, and earn blessings of "health, happy, and prosperity." Light candles, burn incense, maintain altars with relics, photographs, flowers, fruit, and incense sticks.

Many homes and businesses maintain symbols to bring good fortune (aka luck) to the home or business. People in the United States, "one nation under God" perform similar forms of spiritual exercise. On Christmas Eve, people go to church for Midnight mass, people participate in meditation, penance, lighting candles, attending services several times each week, buying spiritual books, attending retreats and other events designed to alleviate stress, sin, depression, and guilt; and many of these measures and others provide a sense of spiritual renewal. All of us want "health, happy and prosperity."

Isn't even just a little bit stunning that America and Americans have so much in common with Vietnam and Vietnamese? Some might deny it; others might make jokes about the possibility. A "first-world country," perhaps the wealthiest country on the planet where all the bells and whistles are within reach of almost everyone, having so much in common with a country and a people that one person said would be "bombed back to the stone age" seems impossible and unimaginable; but, it is true, never-the-less.

Think it Over

Perception is important. Considering perception is vital to being accurate when comparing one person's responses to circumstances and events to our own. Perhaps many of us have not considered, and much less asked about, another person's perspectives about anything of significance. How can people relate to each other well and in a way that honors the Father without accounting for perception?

Ask yourself:

1. Are my perceptions accurate; perceptions about my spouse, each of my children, my other family members, are they on target?

2. What about perceptions related to success, what are mine?

3. How do I perceive people who are different from me, wealthier people, poorer people, destitute people, disabled people, people who are not like me? What about people who are women, men, people of color, well-educated and/or not educated at all?

4. How do I perceive "happy;" what about "health" and "prosperity?"

5. Are my perceptions accurate; are they realistic, are my perceptions hindering?

Chapter 3

What Were We Thinking

"Eye has not seen, nor ear heard, nor have entered into the mind of man [people] the things G has prepared for those who love Him (NKJV)."

"The best laid plans…"

What follows is a series of things that have happened to and through us in Vietnam beginning in 2006.

What a place!

After our first six weeks in Hanoi, Bill becoming a certified teacher of English and Sue experienced being pickpocketed, and both of us making a visit to a "western store" (one that has some familiar items from the "west"), and both of us being shocked after our first visit to Thai Nguyen, the city where we were to live and serve for the next two years, we were both grateful that we had finally arrived and moved in.

It was HOT. It was HUMID. Our room was small, about nine feet wide and about 15 feet long. We had a bathroom, we shared a kitchen with two other American English teachers and with several rats and insects.

We met with the university leadership, an official and formal meeting. We met Mr. Can, the head English lecturer. We also met Mrs. Kim Anh and Ms. Van Anh, two people who worked with international teachers. There were no class schedules, no course assignments, no academic calendars, no class lists, no course books, no curriculum, and no start date for teaching.

Later, much later (years), we found out that there were no plans to have Bill teach, and that the absence of the kinds of information most teachers would expect to receive was standard-operating-procedure! Welcome to Vietnam!

On September 18th, Bill started to teach "English conversation," not really a course, it turned out, just something to give students "exposure to a foreign expert/native speaker of English." Honestly, Bill had no idea what he was doing!

Meet "K 40"

Let the games begin!

In 2006, university level courses were attended by "khoas" or classes of students who all started at the same time and finished four years later. With rare exception, such as a student added to a roster who had "failed" a previous course, the cohort stayed the same, same classes, same tests, same schedules, for four years. Thankfully, "khoas" were divided into smaller groups. For K40 that meant K40A, K40B and K40C, a total of 101 students – six young men and 95 young women. Most, if not all students were from very rural and mountainous areas in northern Vietnam. Some were from small towns near Hanoi, the capital city. Most had taken the national entrance exam and "earned" a place in the University of Education, Thai Nguyen University; but several were recipients of a "scholarship" from their home province. These were given a shot at completing an English education course and were required to teach in their home province after graduating.

Several "qualifiers" – all Vietnamese women looked exactly the same to us. They all had long straight very black hair. Of the 101 students in K40, there were MANY young women students who had the exact same name, first, "middle," and last.

In hindsight, I (Bill) was grateful for the span of time that existed before beginning to teach anyone anything. The first idea came...

Photographs! A verse came to mind, "I have called you by name; you are mine." This was important in at least two ways. First, it was important to decide that these were people we were privileged to serve; and, all of them had names. Second, in a sense, these 101 students, "belonged" to me [us]. Therefore, I wanted to know them and call each one of them by name.

The idea – photograph each student; have each person write what they wanted to be called (not a nickname) above where their head would be in relation to the blackboard. Then, print and cut each picture, print each student's name on a 3x5 card, glue the student's pictures on the card and use the cards to check attendance at the beginning of each class.

101 students divided into three groups of 35, 34 & 32 students. Nguyễn Thị Hà. "Nguyễn," roughly the equivalent of "Jones", except even more common. "Thị" nearly every woman in Vietnam has this as part of her name; and "Hà," a fairly common given name in Vietnamese culture. Nguyễn Thị Trang. "Trang" (sounds like 'chah-ng') is another very common name in Vietnam. We had six, 6, SIX students named Nguyễn Thị Hà; we had six more named Nguyễn Thị Trang; AND, to me, they all looked identical!

Here was our simple solution, put two "Hà's" and two "Trang's" in each group and call them Hà 'A' and Hà 'B', Trang 'A' and Trang 'B'. But, there were other "Hà's" and "Trang's" besides these who had slightly different names, "Nguyễn Thị Minh Trang," for example. This was the beginning of years of a ton of mispronunciation, mistaken identities, and LAUGHTER!

There's more! In our room, the idea of both of us having personal quiet time was pretty funny. Solution: go to my classroom early (unheard of and unprecedented anywhere in Vietnam), and have my quiet time there. While there I would read the Proverb for the day and talk to Father. The 3x5 cards were used to memorize each person's name, learn to associate it with her or his face, and to intercede for each student on the day they were scheduled to be in my class.

Think it Over

How many times have we found ourselves in circumstances and situations where we were faced with things that were drastically and significantly different than what we were expecting? It can be a challenging, even daunting experience. Even something as simple or "common" as how we see and read names: Bill McDonald, first name and last name; Mrs. Sue McDonald. U.S. culture has often "disposed of" a woman's maiden or family name when she marries for many reasons. In Vietnamese culture, a person's family name is read/spoken first, then one or two "middle" names, and then their given name. Obviously, if one were expecting names to be written in the same order as in the U.S., there'd be millions of people with the same given name, "Nguyễn." Though the challenges we have faced are myriad, the blessings received are even more…so stay with us as the story continues.

Ask yourself:

1. What do you expect of and from your spouse? Are those expectations reasonable; have they been discussed with your spouse; does he/she accept those expectations or are hers/his different from the ones you have?

2. What about the expectations you have of and from your child/children? Does the child/do the children even know your expectations; are the expectations the same as they were when they were born; as your child/children get older, do they have an input into what expectations they can fulfill?

3. What about the expectations you have of: God; your co-worker(s), your supervisor at work, your pastor, the teacher(s) of your children and your neighbors?

4. Are there any people in your sphere who you might consider protégé or protégés? Which image would you

associate with those relationships, "slave-driver" or "compassionate teacher;" is there a difference in projecting either one of these or another more appropriate image you are projecting?

Mr. Bill 1st Class, 1st day

Teacher Sue

In the Classroom

Chapter 4

Some Amazing Stuff

"Eye has not seen, nor ear heard, nor have entered into the mind of man [people] the things G has prepared for those who love Him (NKJV)."

Some more things that have happened to and through us in Vietnam.

To many people in the Kingdom, our purpose is simply to "win souls." Some imply that the higher the number of souls "won," the more mature the person "winning" them is; "winning" often indicates that the "winner" has explained and led a "soul" through "the Romans Road", "the Four Spiritual Laws", or some other plan of salvation. A few of these believe and encourage others that it is imperative for the sake of the soul being won (and for the record of the "winner") to be sure to "close the deal." Others maintain that it is sufficient to move a soul along the path to making a decision, at least one step, if not a few, but with the souls going all of the way to a decision.

Organizations follow a line of thinking similar to this "winning souls" idea. In some organizations, the thinking goes something like, "we're here to serve the people and to establish relationships, disciple making relationships where we live and serve." Sometimes these or similar words are explained as being necessary because the organization's financial backers "like" to see that their contributions are making a difference. Of course, and, "difference" = "winning souls," "number of decisions made," "number of Divine encounters" or some other statistic.

Sue and I concluded that, although "winning souls" (meaning people receiving Christ as their Lord and Savior) is a well-meaning and good endeavor, it was not primarily what we came to Vietnam to do. We came to Vietnam, primarily, to teach people English and to establish relationships while doing so. We were confident that as our lifestyle was observed and inquiries made as to what and why that lifestyle was, people would find out about our relationship with the Father, through His Son and how we depend on His Spirit to "get [lead] us through" life. He would "draw people to Himself," as He was "lifted up." And, that's pretty much what's happened.

The Major - Nguyễn Văn Hưng

Hưng is a retired soldier who fought against the French, the Americans, the Chinese, and the Cambodians. Hưng's oldest daughter is Nguyễn Thị Thảo, a student in the K40C group. Thảo comes from a very rural district of a rural province in northern Vietnam. In January 2007, Hưng told Thảo to invite us to his home for the 2007 Tết holiday after finding out that I am a retired American infantryman.

I really did not want to go. Several times I've encountered Vietnamese veterans, typically drunk, who rant on and on about how they "beat" the U.S., et cetera. Tết holiday can be several days long. I did not want to spend several days hearing a lot of "we beat you" stuff. But, in my heart, I wanted to go and so, we went to Nam Dinh Province.

When a foreigner, particularly a white American foreigner goes to a rural village the local "police" come to check you out. This time was no different. The only person who spoke English and Vietnamese was Thảo. After some small talk...I started to share, pretty much as I was given it in my spirit, a list of similarities in the histories of Vietnam and the U.S. There was about 27 items on the list; the "list" was 100% spontaneous, not planned at all. It began with Ho Chi Minh – soldier turned statesman & president and George Washington – soldier turned statesman & president. The last item went: "And then there's those lousy, rotten French!"

Thảo checked to see if I wanted her to translate that, "YES, exactly as I said it," which she then did. The policeman, Hưng, and then everyone else started laughing hysterically. The two Vietnamese men shouting (in Vietnamese), "Yes, yes, those lousy rotten French!" The policeman finished his tea and left. Hưng and I began talking about war, about how professional soldiers do not consider war as something anyone actually "wins." Then, as we were talking, simultaneously, we realized that if our histories, Hưng's and mine, had been different we could have shot each other and none of "this," including Thảo, would have happened. Two old soldiers wept and embraced.

For me, this was turning "swords" into "plows" and we've been friends ever since.

Chinh – the Beggar

The social security and disability systems in Vietnam are very different than anywhere else we've ever been. Disabled people are avoided because "we" might catch whatever is wrong with them. Beggars are largely ignored just because they are beggars and usually filthy; and sometimes they are disabled too.

In 2006 and 2007, we made monthly bus trips to Hanoi. The bus trip took about three hours to travel 45 or 50 miles. Then, we had to catch a city bus to where the "western store" was located.

Back then we went to the bus terminal to get a bus because we did not know another way to do it. At the bus station, there were beggars. One beggar came up to my window and started banging. I stared straight ahead, hoping he'd leave. He did not. Finally, I gave him the 5,000 Vietnam Dong (VNĐ). I heard the Spirit say immediately: "big spender!" 5,000 VNĐ is worth about twenty-five cents! The beggar left and, eventually, we got to Hanoi.

The next trip, the same thing happened. The same beggar was banging on my window. I had felt bad after only giving 5,000

VNĐ and so I doubled it, 10,000 VNĐ (about 50 cents); and yep, I heard Him again…"big spender."

I sought out the Lord, asking what I should do: the next trip, things went differently. We went to the bus and got Sue settled. Then I left to go find that beggar. After finding him, I walked up to him, said hello in Vietnamese and gave him 50,000 VNĐ, about $2.50 but considered unusually large, even by a beggar. Then, I returned to the bus. This became my habit every time we went to the bus station. Then I started carrying a 50,000 VNĐ note folded in my wallet for the beggar if or when I would run into him on the street, which started to happen regularly. I learned that the beggar's name is Chinh (sounds like 'chin'). Chinh is blind in one eye and is lame in one leg. I've never seen Chinh wearing shoes.

Once, Chinh saw me walking down a street long before I saw him. Chinh started to shout, in Vietnamese "Chua ban phuc, Chua ban phuc!" (God bless you, God bless you!). I taught him the English phrase, "shhhh!" After a while, whenever we'd meet, people – shop keepers, office workers, pedestrians, and students in class, nearly everybody – would stop whatever they were doing to watch Chinh and I interact with each other. Then, a spectacular thing started to happen. Townspeople, and some university students, started to give Chinh money out of their pockets!

Now it is 2016, and it has been a few years since I last saw Chinh. I have looked but have not found him anywhere. I hope he's moved on to another city where it is warmer in winter and where people are more giving; but, I fear that he's "gone home." I miss him.

Lệ - the bread lady

In 2008, during the Fall Term, K40 students were in their 4th year and would soon be graduating the following June. I was asked to teach English to 14 teachers from a community college. The goal was for them to take and score well on what is called a TOEFL exam, a very difficult proficiency test in English. These 14 people spoke NO English! Beginning with the Spring Term of 2009, the classes for the group were held at the campus of the new School of Foreign Languages, Thai Nguyen University, located about 3 ½ kilometers away, maybe 4. We lived and I taught on one campus and also taught this group on the other campus. One morning, I was taking a bus to the other campus when I saw a disabled woman. She couldn't walk, and she could not use her right arm or hand. The woman was single-handedly setting up her bread selling spot, in the rain and with no help from her competition. Of course, I had to buy a piece of bread (banh my) from her! A warm baguette that tasted GREAT for 1,000 VNĐ (very cheap!).

Once again, I heard the Spirit: "Make friends with her and someday, pray for her healing." I started buying bread from her every day. At night, it turned out, she would often sell sweet potatoes and corn-on-the-cob off a small hibachi type grill and we would go to her corner and buy some. Lệ speaks no English, but somehow, she understood us, even our terrible Vietnamese or "Vietnam English."

One morning I stopped to buy some bread and showed her a 3x5 card with the words "Hy vong" written on it. "Hy vong" means "hope." Upon looking at the card and hearing me say the word, she said (in Vietnamese) "không có hy vọng," ("Oh no, I have no hope"). I said, "Oh, no big deal, my wife and I have enough for the three of us. Off to teach and more days of buying bread followed.

Once, we celebrated Lệ's birthday (we found the date out somehow) in the street where she was selling bread. Another time, we were getting ready to leave for the U.S. for the summer. We went to a restaurant to take Lệ to lunch, but she would not go in because she knew that the other customers did not want her in there. We talked her into going in for lunch. People DID stare, but no one was rude; and, the owners of the restaurant had a daughter who is deaf. The parents were so happy and thankful that someone was treating a disabled person to lunch in their place that they both wept.

It would take many pages to describe all that has occurred in our relationship with Lệ. I hope this will serve as a sufficient summary.

In the beginning of the 2009 Fall Term, we moved to our new room at the campus where the School of Foreign Languages was located. One day, Lệ came there to see us. After hobbling up the stairs, she collapsed down onto a seat. Then after some initial small-talk she said, "Bill, Bill, be gat oi co hy vong, cam on Bill" (Bill, Bill, now I have hope, thank you Bill!"). Fruit that will remain!

Giang – the Floozie

Giang is what she calls "a modern girl." That means, she wears short skirts, wears make up and basically does what she wants. Giang has never been one who would be confused with a conformist. Giang was a student in K40A. I had determined to stay as far away from her as possible! Of course, she was one of the first students the Spirit started "pestering" me about. Sue and I started with a birthday card. Giang was almost dumbfounded. She had never received a birthday card before. Actually, the date was off by a day or two, but she did not care. That began a relationship that continues into the present day, although Giang no longer resides in Vietnam.

We had been seeking the direction of the Lord regarding several students for us to "focus" on. We sensed and agreed to the number 5 and then prayed over all 101 student names and pictures until we separated five names. These five would be the ones we specifically and regularly would seek to impact, get to know and, maybe even share the Good News with someday. Giang was one of the five.

During one class session, Giang was very sleepy and was sitting near the front so it was rather obvious. During the first break, I sat down on the bench next to her and invited her to go home and get some sleep. Giang looked at me like I was crazy! I repeated myself and added, "Go ahead, the class will still be here next time, go get some rest; it's OK." She couldn't imagine that she was hearing this from a university lecturer. Eventually, she went to her student room, thanking me for the chance to get some rest.

It turned out that Giang had stayed up late the two nights previous studying (cramming) for an exam and really was exhausted. During the class sessions before ours she had been thrown out of the class after being yelled at by the lecturer.

After that day, Giang started to come by our room now and then.

Over the months and years, Sue and I regularly met with "the Five" individually and occasionally altogether. There was no cohesion to the group, per se, and the personalities were extremely varied, to say the least. Sue & I lifted the Five up regularly (daily, and we still do) and when they were about to take final tests after the Spring Term 2007, we asked them if we could pray with all of them for their final tests and the best possible outcomes. They agreed.

One day Giang came to the room. We were close to leaving Vietnam for the summer. Giang said that she would have to quit school and go back to her home town; it was the end of her 3rd year, 2/3rds done! Giang was contacted by her abuser from her childhood. He had abused her for several years. He had AIDS and he wanted her to quit school and come take care of him because, "You probably have AIDS too." To make a long story shorter, Sue went with Giang to Hanoi and had a discreet HIV test done. The nurse agreed to call her the next afternoon with the results, because we lived so far away. At about 2:30 Giang was back in our room, waiting.

Just then a school official decided to visit us and have a chat! Sue took Giang to the common kitchen and I chatted with the official. Suddenly, Giang came by the window doing cartwheels, shouting, and praising and crying! "What's going on, Mr. Bill?" asked the visitor. "I guess she's received some good news," I said.

About a year later, Giang came to us and asked, "Can you tell me how I can become like you; there's something very different about you two and I want to be like that?" Very cautiously and simply, we explained our relationship with the Father. Then, Giang spoke with Father. Fruit that will remain!

Think it Over

Jumping to conclusions: many of us participate in such a pass time. Often, when we see someone, especially if he or she is "different" than we are, we jump to conclusions about lots of things that we have no idea about and, frankly, are usually of no concern of the observer. There's lots of psychobabble available that attempts to describe this phenomenon and offer simple to complex forms of therapy to address underlying issues.

In its most basic form, jumping to conclusions about another person can be funny, truthfully. BUT, it can quickly "morph" into judge mentalism; and THAT can be terrible, ungodly, and somewhere no one really wants to be.

The conclusions I actively jumped to with respect to Giang could have led to us missing a really great and very long-term relationship with one special woman.

Ask yourself:

1. What does the term "floozie" conjure up in your mind; what's the first picture you "see?"

2. There are several groups of people in American society that might be described by some as being "on-the-fringe," e.g. "Goths," "Couch Surfers" and "Gutter Punks." What "groups" do you consider to be "on-the-fringe;" how do you react when you see people who you think are part of one of those groups?

3. Have you ever found out "later" that your conclusions were "off" (i.e. wrong); if so, what did you do about it; what, if anything, would you do differently the next time?

4. What "group" would someone jumping to conclusions about you likely place you into if their conclusions were incorrect?

5. Do you fit any stereotypes?

6. How to you want people to "see" you?

Bill and 'The Major'

Ms. Lệ (Leigh) selling bread

My friend Chien

Giang

Chapter 5

Measurements

"Count the cost..."

"But don't begin until you count the cost. For who would begin construction of a building without first calculating the cost to see if there is enough money to finish it? Luke 14: 28 (NLT)

People perceive success in many ways. The "bottom line" may refer to how much money was made, how many decisions were recorded, how many successfully completed a degree program or even, how many English education majors are teaching English somewhere? We've decided to utilize a very different form of measurement that does not take into consideration any of the criteria mentioned, or any other so-called "bottom line."

We first "signed up" for two years of service, teaching English in Vietnam. TWO YEARS! We were committed to living in a small room, sharing a common kitchen, and enduring the nuances of being a "volunteer English teacher" at a university in Vietnam. We were expecting medals!

Within two or three months after we arrived in Thai Nguyen, we both concluded that staying for just two years would be ineffective. So, we committed to four. I also reneged on a promise I made to Sue and enrolled in a second graduate course, Teaching English to Speakers of Other Languages (our sending organization paid for it, 100% AND the Vietnamese lecturers knew more about the English language than I did!).

How effective is our work in Vietnam, you ask?

In 2006, no one trusted us. Everyone and anyone with any authority expected us to proselytize students; in fact, for many who were doing the same work that WAS priority one. To the people in-charge it was an acceptable cost (dealing with that threat) in exchange for having foreign experts/native speakers teaching their students. There was a Party member in every classroom making sure there was no proselytizing and no subversive communication of any other kind as well.

Frankly, we concluded that our hosts' fears were reasonable, but for a different reason. We were contracted to teach English and to do that well. Some, unfortunately, had made proselytizing the top priority and teaching English a lesser priority. We felt, and still feel, that was ungodly. We had agreed to and were contracted to teach English. We also had agreed NOT to proselytize. We had a problem with justifying violating our word (and the contract) in order to fill up "the bottom line."

Instead, I became very good at teaching English, even to students who had never seen a white guy and had never heard a song sung in English on the radio. And we became very good at building relationships with many, many people, including the monitors in my classrooms.

Sue has taken pictures of nearly 1450 students. We've made cards with their pictures, and hand printed each student's name, in correct Vietnamese language. Further, I've memorized almost all of the names of our students from 2006 to the present.

A lecturer being late to a class session is expected every day, and usually everyday there's a class. "Late" can mean 15 to 60 minutes and then eventually cancelling. I arrive at my classrooms early, sometimes 30 minutes early. Students have learned to be on-time too.

What we would call cheating, Vietnamese students call "helping." It is part of the culture. There are many reasons for this, and we do not need to discuss them here. BUT, we are trying to graduate people who have mastered the language, or at a minimum can write, speak, listen, and read English effectively and accurately.

I've gone so far as to have each person in a classroom of 40 having a different mid-term exam, just so my assessment of their progress was as accurate as possible, and to break the habit of "helping." It works!

In 2015, there is no one who does NOT trust us completely; we're talking from the President of the Province and the President of the university to the sellers in the open market and even our travel agent. We no longer have a class monitor making sure there is no proselytizing; everyone trusts and knows that there is none. Most also know that we are the people to see if there is an issue they need "help" with solving. People have come for "help" when deciding not to return to their hometown, but rather stay in Thai Nguyen. They've come when forced to abort a baby because she was not going to be a boy child. They've come when a marriage is about to take place. Nothing is hidden; many things are done, always with discretion.

Just a few hours before we left Vietnam for a two-month summer break (June 2015), we were given official, temporary resident status and cards; we no longer require a visa to enter the country.

Our work, our lifestyle, our time in Vietnam has been and is effective.

Think it Over

Many of us who grew up in the U.S. have had success dangling in front of our faces for a long time. For many, it isn't until we reach the late 50's or later that we realize that success, as it was dangled, was not necessarily the best thing to be pursued. Many in Vietnam apply for scholarships to study abroad somewhere in the world. They write letters they get recommendations, they assemble a resume, they get interviewed but, many times, they do not get selected. Most often an applicant who did not get the scholarship that was applied for says: "I failed!" That is not true (usually); usually someone else was picked. Not achieving a desired outcome, whether that is a scholarship to study abroad or a goal to become the president and CEO of a reputable corporation, does not necessarily equal failure. The opposite of success is not always failure.

For us, we discovered rather quickly that we needed to recalculate how we were going to measure our success in serving people in Vietnam.

Ask yourself:

1. In whatever you are doing at this time in your life, what is the best way to determine whether or not you are experiencing success?

2. Does your method of assessment work; is the way you see success tougher on yourself than how you measure someone else's success?

3. When success eludes you is "I've failed" your default response?

Chapter 6

For the Duration

"I am with you always, even until the end of time;" I'll never leave you nor forsake you (NIV)."

"It ain't over 'til it's over."

We were fired! In 2005, we had been working with first-time single moms for about three years. I was about to change my commercial driver's license to an Illinois license. I had begun the process of getting licensed and certified as a social worker in the same state but suddenly, it was over.

Soon, we were sitting in our home in Missouri with Sue asking, "What are we going to do now?" Meaning, "Where are we going to get money from?" We decided to seek direction from Father for a month.

At the end of 30 days, we sat together and shared what we'd each heard/sensed/gotten from our time of inquiry. I had heard, "Go to Vietnam and teach English." Because I had earned a graduate degree, I was eligible to teach and to be accompanied by my "non-teaching spouse." Sue's response was: "I'm not going to Vietnam; you can go, but I'm not going."

We agreed to continue to pray and seek Father's direction for a year, and at the end of the year, if Sue could not "hear" or "see" God in it, we would not go. We made a list of 20-something things that would have to occur in order for Sue to even consider that God might be in this idea. We started to pray; then, we started to check off the things on that list. In July 2006, we were on our way to Thai Nguyen, Vietnam – together. We had "signed up" for two years.

Two years…frankly, we were thinking like a married couple who had been overseas with the military and so we had images of "short-timer's" calendars on our wall, even before we left! Neither one of us has ever been imprisoned, but we were thinking that "this" (these next two whole years, living in one small room) was our "bit of suffering" in the Kingdom. Break out the marching band and parades in our honor!

We'd been looking forward to going to Honduras. There were many reasons, not the least of which was comfort; we were comfortable there; we had friends there; we could ALMOST speak the language there! I had argued with God almost as vehemently as Sue had initially objected. But then, as I was presenting my case to the Lord one more time, I could see in my "heart's eye" the image a mentor of mine had shared years earlier. He saw a rock, representing Jesus Christ, the Rock, dropping onto and into Honduras and the ripples, representing the Good News, reverberating around the world, from Honduras. I could see one of those ripples touching Vietnam; then, I was looking at a world map and noticed that Honduras and Vietnam are at the same latitude on the globe! I was hooked.

There are just a few words of English that can cause a real stir and get somebody's attention quicker than you'd want to (it turns out); one word is Jesus, as in the Christ, and the other is, what we sometimes call it in Vietnam, the 'M' word (MISSIONS). Those might be referred to as "fire starters." We referred to ourselves as "CET's," as in Christian English Teachers, which is what we were, are and what was requested when the Vietnamese first contacted our sending organization!

I "cut my teeth" doing evangelism on-the-street in New Orleans, Louisiana during Mardi Gras in 1986. After 20 years of serving people in New Orleans and other places, including in Honduras, I thought (and I fear that many of "us" do too), that "M-work" is just evangelism 24/7 – 365 days a year. I was sure that I was the gift to the sending organization's vision, meaning all others were not in the same league. It's called pride and it nearly scuttled the work before it had a chance to get started.

Fortunately, Dave Munson was correct back in 1986 when he said, "If your wife ever decides to be led by the Spirit, she'll pass you by almost instantly;" she did and she has. Sue said it first, but we both realized quickly that we were never going to make a dent in Vietnam in just two years. We decided then and there to commit to four years and for me to enroll in a graduate course in teaching English to speakers of other languages. Why, some might ask? Because the Vietnamese considered us the experts, the native speakers of English. The Vietnamese lecturers knew more about English than we did. And, we believed that I had to equip myself to get as close to meeting that expectation as possible. Plus, since we committed to four years, the sending organization paid for the graduate course (but, honestly, that did not make up for the grief of doing another graduate degree!).

August 2006 – June 2008, if we would have stayed with that plan we would have been leaving just as the students had started. During that time, we learned names, fed "western" food and interceded for our students and we watched we them became proficient with English and teaching, as they finished their third year of university! How could we have done that and then tell them, in effect, "so long," "fare-thee-well," "blessings to you and yours".... "it's been nice?"

We were in a unique situation; one that our usually much younger team members couldn't enjoy, simply because they were too young. We started to develop relationships with senior administration officials. Often, an official would ask for help with their English and take correction and advice well because, we sensed, we were more like peers. The whole "losing face" thing was never an issue. Age is respected in Asia.

No one has ever said this publicly that I know of, but it does seem that some think that Vietnamese people are ignorant (to put it mildly). It is true, ignorance and stupidity know no borders, but neither does common sense. "Everyone" knew that most of the "volunteer teachers" were very temporary at best, rarely fully committed to staying longer than a contract with some enduring four years. Virtually none of the "volunteer teachers," save the leadership of the sending organization, knew many of the faculty or any of the administration or the system of education. It occurred to us that the leadership of the university knew precisely the reasons behind the desire to teach in Vietnam and that they guarded against those reasons becoming a problem. The worse part, no leader that I know or have known counted on any of the "volunteer teachers" being there for anything resembling "long-term."

They all do now.

In June 2012, we were required to take a "home assignment." After seven years in Thai Nguyen, our financial situation was in trouble, approximately -$11,600 in trouble. We believed that we would be able to "raise" the amount plus the several thousand required to finance the next "go round" and commitments for the next years' financial support as well. We assured the leadership of the Faculty of Foreign Languages, Thai Nguyen University that we would be back, in Thai Nguyen and at the school ready-to-teach, on August 1st, 2013. Our organization did not share our enthusiasm or our optimism. Our "handler" (the person tasked with managing our financial profile) estimated 18 months. February 2013, our account deficit reached $0! But, the organization still wanted us to do some things that would require us to stay in the U.S. for up to 18 months or more. There would be no assurance that we'd be returning to the same school or even the same city; BUT, we'd promised (in faith) – August 1st, 2013.

Back up! During the year + June 2012 – August 1st, 2013, we were planning on making visits to many places, many groups of people, several large gatherings to talk about our life in Vietnam and ask for the participation of as many who would help us financially in our work in Vietnam. At the start of what became 37,000 miles of driving and another 3,000 traveled by air, we stopped at the headquarters of a rather large "like-minded" organization. The executive staff of this group had been interceding for us on a regular basis and we wanted to visit and provide the staff an update. But, first we had to go through a display illustrating and explaining that organization's origin and method of operation.

This organization, from the first initial contact made with a people group who has invited the organization to help them, commits to investing between 15 to 20 years into that people group. It is worth emphasizing: 15 to 20 YEARS! Remember, initially we had committed to TWO years. This organization commits to TWO DECADES! We were stunned, to put it mildly, and a little embarrassed. We were also motivated.

A frequent phrase used during World War II says: "For the duration." It meant soldiers, sailors and U.S. Marines were in it, the war, until it was finished, over and won. Shortly after our visit to this interceding partner of ours, we adopted the phrase to our life and work in Vietnam, and specifically to Thai Nguyen and the School of Foreign Languages, "for the duration;" meaning for between 15 to 20 years.

Two factors effected our calculation of what exactly "the duration" would entail. First, we had started with K40 back in 2006. The School of Foreign Languages started in 2008 with a small group of transferred students designated K30. In September 2017, the School of Foreign Languages will welcome the freshman class of K40; the four-year students of that class will graduate in June 2021. Second, in 2020, we both will celebrate our 65th birthdays; but, we cannot leave the second K40 ½ way through their 4th Year. That means, we are committed to staying in Thai Nguyen, Vietnam at the School of Foreign Languages (hopefully by then the University of Foreign Languages) until the four-year students of K40 graduate in June of 2021. June of 2021 will mark the end of our 15th year of teaching English in Thai Nguyen University.

What comes after June 2021? We don't know. However, we do think that our affiliation with the School/University will continue, perhaps in the form of several visits each year, but we will consider that in the future.

In 2013, we made the decision, after much praying, to return to Vietnam and "our" school and city "on our own," that is without the sponsorship of an approved non-government organization. As it turns out, the decision was a good one. The organization we initially came to Vietnam with decided to leave Thai Nguyen within a year after we returned!

And this year, 2015, we became official temporary residents of Vietnam. We've been issued what we call "Vietnamese Green Cards" that are renewable in two years. We are now officially here for the duration!

Think it Over

Let's face it; the age we live in is not very conducive to doing anything for a very long time. People live in many different places, work at several jobs and more than just a few marry a few different people during their lifetime. In general, it seems, few people take time, for anything. Perhaps a better way to express it: "few people take MUCH time for anything these days." Why is that?

The phenomenon, if it is that, may not be intrinsically bad; it is certainly not "evil." However, it may be the cause for eliminating some words from the English language, words such as "savor" and phrases such as "'til the cows come home" or "to the moon and back." While compared to other issues, taking time may not register as an issue; we think it is closer to travesty than it is to a good thing.

Ask yourself:

1. How does waiting "too long" in a drive-thru lane at a fast-food place effect the rest of your day?

2. Can you list two long-term projects, jobs, relationships, or commitments that you are currently involved in and have been for a "long" time?

3. If you had trouble making the list in #2, what do you think is the reason for that inability?

4. What exactly do you consider to be a "long" time?

5. If our children spend a majority of their time at school, and if both parents are working and so either not-at-home or wasted when they are home, if time spent with our children is an entry on our day planners, are we parenting or are we housing and providing board?

6. Our Creator would like to enjoy a relationship with each of us for eternity; how long is that, and, can you commit to a relationship for that long?

Helping a teacher out

Mrs. Sue talking with students

Praying with the Five!

Chapter 7

Confirmation

"Do not receive an accusation against an elder except **from two or three witnesses** (NKJV)."

"Even so, every good tree bears good fruit... (NKJV)."

There may be some who enjoy wasting time; that is, there may be people to whom the effectiveness of whatever they are doing does not matter. There are, of course, other people who manipulate all sorts of factors so that what they are doing seems to matter or appears to be extremely effective. Perhaps happiness and genuine contentment is between these two "bookends."

With a commitment to live, work and relate to people for 15 years we did not want to wait until the 15 years are over, and then try to decide whether or not we've been effective.

What follows are occurrences that we have welcomed along the way and treasured as indicators that we were on "the right track." As best as I can remember, they are written in chronological order, and one occurrence may open the door to others.

We had been forewarned that a "monitor" would be in the classrooms to ensure that nothing that violated the laws of Vietnam was being said or discussed. Additionally, I had seen first-hand how saying the wrong things at the wrong time, especially in the presence of the wrong person could get someone deported or jailed. So, on September 12th, 2006 – my first class session at the University of Education in Thai Nguyen – I was determined to not violate any laws!

I was nervous. I had no idea what to start with. I had no curriculum, no lesson plan, no idea what I was supposed to be teaching the students of K40A. So, of course, I decided to begin my class by introducing myself, in Spanish.

These were 2nd year students and, as I soon discovered, many of them were fairly high-level speakers of English already. No one was sure that I was NOT speaking English but none of the things I spoke was understood by anyone. Thus, there were many wide eyes and mouths hanging open. Out of respect for the foreign expert and university lecturer, and not wanting me to "lose face," nobody wanted to be first to admit they did not recognize ANY of what I was saying, no one was about to ask "Teacher, what the heck are you talking about?" In the front row was a young woman from Ha Nam, a town not far from Hanoi. The girl's name was Linh. Finally, she slowly raised her hand and when I called on her she asked: "Teacher...is that English you are speaking?" "English," I said, "You want to study English? I thought you wanted to learn Spanish!" And then I started to introduce myself and began to engage with this group of 27 (of 35 assigned to the group) sophomore students of English Education.

Then, it happened: "Does anyone have any questions for me? I promise I will answer almost any question anyone wants to ask; so, who has a question?" SILENCE. More silence; and, still more silence. Finally, a small hand could be seen appearing above someone's head. "Yes," I asked.

"Teacher, why did you and your wife decide to come to Vietnam?" Remember the incendiary words...what was I going to give as our reason? Then I heard inside my head, "Remember, if you deny Me, I'm denying you; but, if you speak up for Me, I'll take care of you (NLT)." Visions of immediate deportation emerged. Who is the monitor, I thought?

I went on to explain, "we are both what are called 'born-again Christians' and that means for us that we believe that Jesus Christ is Lord and we don't do anything unless we believe it to be His will for us. So, we spent over a year praying and asking Him what we should be doing next (referring to our termination in 2005) and we believe that it was His will for us to sell everything we owned and come to Vietnam and teach all of you English so that you are all at least as fluent in English as we are."

Silence. I waited for a reaction. Would the monitor finally identify her or himself; would people listening from another location burst in and arrest me? Silence; and then many of the students just said: "WOW!" Frankly, I nearly wept.

Then we continued to introduce ourselves to each other until Sue came and, after introducing her to the class, she began taking pictures of each student and then the entire group.

Three of those class members soon became part of "the Five" and our close relationship with them, and the other three as well, continues to the present. One of those class members was Giang, mentioned earlier; she and another student have made confessions of faith in the Lord.

In the next two days, the same thing occurred with K40 B and K40 C. With the response being the same, "WOW!"

Personally, I do not believe that I had much influence on the quality of anyone's English. However, this group of 101 students most likely concluded that once our two years was done they'd never see either one of us again. The fact that most of them have seen us or communicated with us via e-mail, or Facebook or telephone, was a welcomed surprise. One student in that very first group eventually confided with us that her Mom required open-heart surgery. Her family could not afford the operation and asked us if we could pray. We did, and it was soon determined that her mother did not need the surgery, but that through establishing some healthy parameters and staying committed to a simple regimen of medicine, she would have a good life; and, she has and still does!

The same student, within a short time after graduation, was diagnosed with Hepatitis B, a very common and usually fatal disease in Vietnam. She was embarrassed and kept her diagnosis a secret; but she wanted to tell us and ask if we would pray for her because, "I remember what happened to my Mom." And so, we began to intercede and now she is healthy, married, and expecting her first child.

Another student, one of three boys in one group, graduated and began teaching in the mountainous region of his province. Our School is the Regional Center for English Education training in the Northern Mountainous Region of the country and as such supports thousands of English teachers from rural areas in their teaching and in improving their English skills. During one session at our School, the young man heard a familiar voice as he was climbing the steps to the third floor; it had been four years since graduation, but here was Mr. Bill! He was stunned that we were still in Vietnam and still in Thai Nguyen.

Time and space restrictions prevent the detailed accounts of many similar stories; the woman whose first question to us in 2006 was "Mr. Bill why do you and your wife always hold hands; and, why do we hear you saying, 'I love you' to each other so much? This is very unusual in our country for people your age." The woman asking was one of the "Ha B's." In 2010, Sue and I went to Ha B's wedding. She wanted us there because she wanted her marriage to be like ours, and she hoped by us coming it would help that to happen. Ha B is a high school English teacher and she brings her classes to Thai Nguyen once a year. During those visits, she and Sue get together.

Ms. Dung, a primary school English teacher from Cao Bang, near the border with China loves to eat, and really loves Mrs. Sue's Christmas cookies. We still send or bring a batch to her every Christmas. Dung was also a teacher-student at our school and recently acquired the highest credential of proficiency in English.

Trang 'A' is now a well-known and extremely talented high school English teacher who we see often. Many semesters we will travel to the high school where she teaches, spending an entire day working and socializing with her, her students, and colleagues.

Another, the daughter of my retired soldier friend, is now my colleague and teaching university English at the University of Sciences. We see her, her husband and baby often.

These stories and the thousands not told serve as evidence of the ministries effectiveness. Specifically, we have found favor with...men [people]. Our first group, however, K40, and especially what's come out of that first session and answering the question, "Why" has resulted in developing uniquely dynamic and thoroughly trusting relationships with most of that initial group of 101. Literally, thousands of other students, teachers, administrators and so many other people in our community are our dear friends.

We've been confirmed! The verse, alluded to earlier, comes from the Story as written by Luke. It reads in its entirety, "Also I say to you, whoever confesses Me before men [people], him the Son of Man also will confess before [the Father]. But he who denies Me before men will be denied before [the Father] (NKJV)." And in another place it reads..."Let not mercy and truth forsake you; bind them around your neck, write them on the tablet of your heart, and so find favor and high esteem in the sight of God and man [people] (NKJV)."

Charles Haddeus Spurgeon wrote, in part: "we must not tie Him [the Lord] down to one mode of operation[1]." To be specific, Spurgeon wrote this in a different context, but the truth can be applied to many areas of life in Christ, ours included.

There have been many experiences that we have had or observed where the "mode of operation" was different from what we would have expected or even accepted. For us, the "foundation" of our service to the specific Vietnamese people we serve and to the community, even the entire country is made up of several truths that we have adopted and choose to specifically accept as being TRUE. Here are a few of them:

---

[1] Spurgeon, C.H. (1997,2002) Morning and Evening, Whitaker House New Kensington, PA, USA

- "And I, if I am lifted up, will draw all [people] unto Myself (NKJV)."

- "So is My word be that goes forth from My mouth; it shall not return to me empty, BUT it shall accomplish what I desire, it shall [PROSPER] in the thing for which I sent it (NIV)."

- "So..., whatever you do, do all to the glory of God (NIV)."

- "Be REAL guys!"

(all emphasis added)

And, walking it out in real and everyday life...

- A very senior administration official informed me that there was a diagnosis of a brain tumor with a 99% chance of dying and a 1% chance that if death does not come, talking and walking will still be impossible. I blurted out, "Oh no! In Jesus' name that will not happen!" "Oops," I said, "I forgot where I was." Right after I left the office, I contacted people all over the world who prayed that this does not happen and that this tumor will be taken care of." The official had the tumor surgically removed and was able to both walk and talk. At the 45th anniversary celebration of a university there in our city, the official's wife approached us and said, "Thank you, I know that you were praying for my husband."

- A colleague, a woman, walked up, introduced herself and began to talk about a possible scholarship to complete her graduate program in Hawai'i. After a few minutes, I assured her to "go pack your bags, you're going." About a year later, she returned and she shared her experience. After a few minutes, I suggested that she should pursue a doctorate degree, if she intended to make university education a career. She does, but asks, "Why;" I say, "because you see this campus? I "see" you being in-charge of all of this someday; I believe you'll be the first woman university president in the country." She laughed. May 2012, right before we left for the U.S. she moved into her new office as the new Vice-Dean of the School of Foreign Languages.

- In June 2009, K40 graduated from the University of Education. An amazing 60% of the graduates have secured employment as teachers by August 2006.

- In May 2012, I finished the term teaching first-year students from K34. We were leaving soon for about a year in the U.S. and so we invited every student we've ever had to come to the last Library Night; hundreds come. The room is too small and the conversations moved out to the balcony where one freshman girl was on the verge of tears: "Mrs. Sue," she says, "this is too much for me, I cannot understand anything anyone is saying." Sue: "Just listen, don't try to say anything. Don't worry; soon you'll be speaking just like these or even better." In June 2015, she graduated after, among other things, coming to one of my classrooms to encourage a new cohort of freshman to not give up, to trust us to help them get to where she now stands and even further along!

- Six years ago, Lệ became a single-parent. In our "western contaminated" mindset about "winning souls," I chalked her up as a "loss." However, late one night, just after secretly conducting "dunking" of a new "C-creature," there was a loud and hard banging on the outside door; Sue and I both said: "BUSTED!" It was Lệ. Because we had a person in our room who could interpret, we were given the sad and desperate story that led to the decision to ask a man to "give me a baby." After hearing the whole thing, Sue and I were crying, everyone was crying, and we committed ourselves (Sue & I did) to helping Lệ raise this baby. In June 2015, Lương, who turns six years old in August, begins English language classes for 6-year-olds in the English Learning Center for kids located on the ground floor of the building where our flat is located!

- In the open-market where we buy our food, there was one woman who sold fruit. Her stand was very close to where I bought "ném," a very unhealthy but really good tasting Vietnamese fried springroll. One day, she told Sue, through an interpreter, that she was dying from Type II diabetes. Sue has Type II diabetes. She proceeded to tell the woman what to do to take care of her diabetes and maintain a normal life. The woman took Sue's advice and is still selling fruit. We eventually moved to another area of the city and a different open-market. In 2015, we are strolling in the city center looking at all of the sights there because Tet is about to happen when that woman, still very healthy and happy, bumps into us and becomes ecstatic over seeing Sue (and both of us) again after a long time. Tết is the name for the Lunar New Year celebration that occurs in Vietnam, and several other countries, annually. The full name of the first day of the holiday is "**Tết Nguyên Đán**" which means "the Morning of the First Day" in Vietnamese language. Tết is a great time focusing on family reunion, starting off the new year with a "clean slate," and lots of food, parties, and friends! Unfortunately, many people, Americans in particular, only recognize Tết when connected to the 1968 Tết Offensive during the war in Vietnam. The truth is, the good things about Tết vastly outweigh that grisly part of history. For more information on Tết, go to https://en.wikipedia.org/wiki/Tết on-line.

- Then there's the other senior university official who, with his wife, named us his daughter's "second parents," at her and her husband's wedding ceremony and asked us to "speak to them" before they left for the groom's family home.

- Finally, we have a travel agent who issues us airline tickets destined for anywhere before we pay; why? Because "there is no one like you two, who have given up their life in the U.S. to come and live in Vietnam to help so many Vietnamese people"....and the cavalcade of "confirmations" continues even up until now!

Another part of our "foundation" states: "A man's [person's] gift makes room for him and brings him before great men [people] (NASB)." "Great" = every one of our students, our colleagues, our leaders in the university and in the government, the shop keepers, the market vendors, the beggars, and so many others that we get to interact with where we live.

Think it Over

God really is "no respecter of persons." What is on your heart that comes from Him and that seems "crazy" or "wild," OK, even a little insane? What "confirmations" would you like to see and experience? What kinds of things would help to affirm that you were in the right place at the right time? Many times, I've concocted some scheme and started to operate in that scheme and "confirmation" was nowhere to be found. As you read and perhaps re-read these "confirmations" or "evidences," I wonder, what would confirmations look like to you in the context of whatever is on your heart?

Chapter 8

Cost

"I will not offer to God…that cost me nothing (NIV)."

"Truly I tell you, this poor widow has put more into the treasury than all the others. They all gave…but she…put in everything—all she had to live on." Matthew 12:43 & 44 (NIV)

There was a time when almost every boy in my neighborhood dreamt of being a big-league ballplayer. Growing up in the capital of baseball, it was easy to have that dream…c'mon; there were three great teams to "choose" from.

Our youngest son caught the bug…he thought he wanted to become a major leaguer. Neither of us had any clue what that would cost. One summer he went to Mickey Owen's Baseball School in southcentral Missouri. I asked a coach about the odds of making it to the "bigs" and this is what he told me:

Think of the number of boys who play baseball in every high school in the U.S. Now, about 1 % of them are good enough to play for a university; now a boy who was the only guy in is town, or county throwing a baseball near 90 miles per hour is one of four or five guys who are throwing at 90 miles an hour and faster. Now, about 1% of that 1% turns professional, meaning they get paid to play baseball; and, out of that 1% make it to the major leagues.

Things were looking grim!

As I stated earlier, and to reiterate a bit, we had just finished our three-year tenure working with single women who were first-time moms. Our ending was rather sudden and unexpected but, in hindsight, it turned out well. Sue had asked, "So, what are we going to do now?" Which is code for, "Where are we going to get any money to live on?"

I suggested praying for 30 days and hearing what the Lord had to say. Sue agreed (but also found a job) and we sought the will of our Father for a month. Then, thirty days later, almost to the minute, Sue asked, "So, what have we been hearing?"

Time out! Do not think *for even a moment* that Sue did not seek God and His direction for our life. Don't think *for a split second* that Sue's faith was weak or anything similar. Sue is a woman of faith.

By the time she asked the question, almost 12 years had passed since my retirement from the United States Army. I retired in order to "go into ministry full-time." We had lost a house we had bought because I was "sure" we would be in Kansas for the rest of our lives; I had dug a hole of debt so deep, partly because of my expecting God to finance my ideas. I imagined He would bless (and pay for), my ideas: but all we saw for our efforts was debt.

I sensed God leading us to go to Vietnam, to teach English at a university, with Sue serving as a "non-teaching spouse." "You can go to Vietnam and teach if you want to, but I'm *not* going!" Wait, I'm the spiritual head of this family…AND, I was about to evoke a "Gibbs' Rule" that I had misused a thousand times before. BUT THEN…

Delay of Game! Some guys will be thinking, "Wait, she is *supposed* to honor [or respect or submit to or obey] her husband; he *is* the spiritual head…she *should've* said 'Yes, dear' and followed whatever you heard."

In August of 1985, I survived the second of two very nearly fatal parachute jumps. I had jumped on August 17th and I sort of woke up sometime early on August 21st. I sustained three ruptured blood vessels in my brain, resulting in nine grand mal seizures. It was my last parachute jump.

God used that experience to get my undivided attention, which I committed to giving, "100% for the rest of my life."

So, fast-forward to February 1986, on my first trip to street witness at Mardi Gras in New Orleans, Louisiana. On the way back, God used a man, Mr. Dave Munson, to tell me that He (God) "did not like the way I was treating His little girl." I was stunned and immediately began to learn how to be a husband in a way that was pleasing to God first, trusting that she, my wife, would eventually welcome a man who was husbanding in a way approved by God.

In a school bus, traveling north on I 57, I started. I found where God says, "Husbands, love your wives, even as Christ also loved the church, and gave himself for it (NKJV)." Of course, that verse is just after that frequently misquoted *club-verse*, "Therefore, as the church is subject unto Christ, so let the wives be to their own husbands in everything (NKJV)."

Immediately, it came to me: "*gave* himself? He *died* for the church, I've never given myself to Sue like that, for her benefit; I've only given to her to get what I deserve from her anyway." Actually, I had never given myself to anyone; I had gotten comfortable with people giving to me and me taking from people. That was all about to change.

BUT THEN…the Spirit got hold of me, right there sitting together in front of our fireplace and something very different and unexpected (from Sue's perspective, and mine) happened.

I said:

Hey, I am supposed to be the spiritual leader of our family, right? So, maybe I am hearing from the Lord what He wants us to do next. How about we pray for one year; then, after one year, if you cannot hear God in this, we won't go; even if we are walking down the walkway to the plane, if you say you cannot hear God in this, I promise, we will turn around and not go.

To say that Sue was a tad skeptical would be a gross understatement; she had heard similar promises before. But, this time, God was leading, not me!

It actually took 14 months; on July 31st, 2006, we were on our way to Thái Nguyên, Việt Nam.

Oh, the *cost*…so far it has cost – me learning how to spiritually lead, which included learning to become humble enough to put Sue first ("[Love]…is not self-seeking," 1 Corinthians 13:5, NIV).

- Asking permission (to get the blessing) of each of our parents and children for us to go to Vietnam.

- Us selling nearly everything we owned and putting what was left in an 8X8 storage shed.

- Sue trusting God when she sensed Him say, "It's OK, go."

- Us being here in Vietnam when each of our Dad's died.

- Our first three-months stipend lost to a pickpocket in Hanoi.

- Us not seeing our grandchildren for (up to) 10 years of their lives.

- Neither of us seeing our Mom's much except once a year.

- Very, very little to no corporate fellowship.

- Having to learn a new way of communicating the Good News without getting into legal problems, thrown in jail, or deported.

- Having to get acclimated to a very different climate, a very different calendar, a very different daily schedule, very different kind of food, a very different way of buying food, a very different kind of language, a very different teaching environment (electricity going off w/o notice, classroom with no heat, no sound equipment, students, and lecturers coming to class VERY late, and blatant cheating called "helping").

We made a list of things, issues, that had to be settled and/or eliminated in order, before we could go; these are some of those things:

- Debts that had to be paid.

- Decisions about property.

- Acquiring 12 month prescriptions of all medications.

- Acquiring financial support to a level required by our "sending organization."

- Getting the OK from our families.

- The care and upkeep of our house and property.

- The care of what was left of our stuff in the 8X8 storage shed.

- Being accepted by the sending organization.

- Sue feeling confident that Father was sending us, BOTH of us to Vietnam.

All of the things that had to be met were met. With no badgering or checking, Sue eventually agreed to go! And, finally, the problem of getting a 12-month prescription filled was solved with the assistance of the United States Air Force!

Frankly, the cost has been high. In many ways, it sometimes feels too costly; but then, we are blessed, ABUNDANTLY!

We have had and continue to have an amazing amount of favor with people in virtually every social and economic status in our community. Many people have been affected personally in various ways that we identify collectively as "life," those things that most people need to enjoy a fairly comfortable existence, i.e. good job, health, and life in general, here, and now; and a few have been affected with "life more abundantly" and look forward to an eternity of joy unspeakable and peace that surpasses understanding!

We have and do consider the costs and we have found that the price we pay, in many ways that it is paid, well worth what we see as results. GLORY TO HIM!

Think it over

1. In what areas of life has God asked for your 100%, undivided attention regarding?

2. In how many areas of your life are you committed to completing it/them in a God approved and God pleasing way?

3. Are you the spiritual leader of your family; how well has that been going?

4. What is it costing you to NOT be 100% committed to the Lord in every area of life?

5. What is it costing people that depend on you for you to NOT be 100% committed to the Lord in every area of life?

6. What would it take for you to be 100% committed to the Lord in every area of life?

7. What would it be like for the people in your life if you were to be 100% committed to the Lord in every area of life?

8. Are you submitted to your spouse; are you giving yourself for your spouse as Christ gave Himself for the Church?

9. What does that look like; what would that look like?

Chapter 9

Expectations

"...my expectation is from Him (NKJV)."

List all of the expectations you have [there were about 51]; now, draw a line through every one of the expectations that you cannot personally guarantee the outcome of. (There were TWO without a line drawn through them!)

There is no commandment that states, *"thou shall not have any unreasonable expectations."* Neither is there any commandment forbidding our possession of self-seeking expectations, ungodly expectations, unrealistic expectations, or any unspoken expectations either! There is, however, solid advice about avoiding anger, worry, and confusion; all of which can and do often come, as a result of, expectations.

I was expecting some things when we landed in Hanoi, Vietnam. Sue wasn't expecting anything.

I expected to be treated like a visiting dignitary. I expected heat; it is a tropical climate, after all. I expected secret police eavesdropping on us (although I really wasn't sure who "us" was, exactly). I was expecting to be a covert evangelist; I was expecting clandestine operations under blankets, using small flashlights and singing using sign language for the deaf. I was expecting Vietnamese people to be waiting, lined up so-to-speak, for me to give them each a word of truth!

I was expecting a teaching schedule. I was expecting coordination between us and "them," them being the officials who had asked specifically for born-again Christians, who were college educated and whose first language was English. I was expecting a classroom with good lighting, a sound system and even a language lab, maybe. I was expecting my U.S. colleagues to be like-minded which for me meant, have the same theology; including opinions consistent with mine about leading someone to faith, disdain for the Easter bunny, Santa Claus, and Easter egg hunts. I expected identical feelings about alcohol and tobacco use and mirror opinions about sex outside of marriage, marriage being between one man and one woman for life, even though some (OK, many) go through divorce and remarriage. I expected an identical passion for bringing a person to faith! I expected all of us to maneuver from "How do you say _ _ _ _" to "Would you like to pray to receive Christ," as quickly as possible (after all Christ's return is imminent, isn't it???).

I was wrong[2]!

Expectations are a lot like promises, some promises anyway; they get broken. Another expectation I'd had was that the officials were not smart enough to understand what we were actually intending to do, which was, to see people come to faith in Christ. I was wrong about that, too!

This place we call Vietnam has had a history full of betrayal and war. Much war instigated by nations that had expressed some sort of connection or a desire for relationship; only for the relationship to deteriorate into usury and war.

Why would anybody in their right mind expect that any group of people would be content with people who first presented themselves as friends, only to eventually collect the rice they had grown and charge the growers for that rice; rice that they had grown and were harvesting?

Why would anybody in their right mind expect that any group of people would be happy with a people who first presented themselves as friends but who would eventually colonize their

---

[2] Phrase borrowed from the title of the book: I Was Wrong: The Untold Story of the Shocking Journey from PTL Power to Prison and Beyond, Bakker, J. October 1997; Thomas Nelson Publishing

land, institute its own government and hierarchy and even change the language spoken by the people of that native group?

Americans have enjoyed an absence of war on their soil, beginning with the end of the Civil War until the terrorist attacks in 2001. Vietnam had experienced war, on their soil, at least once every ten years in every decade from the 14th Century until the end of the first decade of the 21st Century! The Portuguese came as friends, the French and Americans came as friends, the Chinese were (and are) neighbors! Ho Chi Minh quoted the American Declaration of Independence while declaring independence from France as he was surrounded by several American OSS agents on September 2nd, 1945! Given all their experience with so-called friends, why would any Vietnamese person or government trust anyone, especially anyone from one of those groups or anyone who claimed to be a friend?

Vietnam and many Vietnamese people claim to be a people of relationship; actions speak otherwise. Many times, people cut in front of each other to be first, or because someone is not moving as quickly as they would like. Based on past experience of the nation as a whole, why wouldn't most Vietnamese people have given up on the idea of relationships?

We did not, I didn't at least, expect to have to make relationships the old-fashioned way; *we've had to earn them.*

Adjustments needed to be made in the expectations we had; we needed to change more than just a few things. Here are but a few of the changes we faced.

Change #1. We were asked to *teach English*, not to teach a few cute English phrases found in the Good News New Testament and use that as a way to secretly proselytize Vietnamese students! *That* would be using our faith to rationalize or justify lying, breaking our agreement which was to, teach English to university students in Vietnam.

Change #2. The Vietnamese characterized us as EXPERTS; English is, after all, our first language. I had to become an expert or at least a lot closer to being an expert than I was when we first arrived. Most Vietnamese lecturers of English still know more about the technicalities of English than I, and maybe most Americans, do (with the possible exceptions of Mr. Bergen or Mr. Berkey, two English teachers I had in junior and senior high school). I went back to graduate school and earned certification and a degree in teaching English to people who speak other languages (TESOL).

Change #3. Many authority figures in Vietnam presume that American Christians are up to no good; we are trying to subvert Vietnamese lifestyle and culture. They often see Christianity as "Western", meaning something that they are not (although when we fly to Vietnam we actually fly west! So, actually, they are the West!). To change that perception, we, in essence, became Vietnamese (almost).

Some Vietnamese men believe that to be a Vietnamese man you must drink a lot of alcohol and have at least one mistress. A long, uncut fingernail on one's pinky is another important trait. The pinky is supposed to prevent displaying the image of an ordinary laborer. The mistress adultery is used to satisfy the lust of men of any culture who cannot or will not control themselves. Mistresses are not exclusive to Vietnamese culture; but, long pinky nails pretty much are. There are all sorts of charades men all over the world perform to broadcast their masculinity; from tattoos, to mirror sunglasses, to smoking non-filter cigarettes, to driving recklessly fast. Many of us do some pretty dumb things to make ourselves appear as "real men" and impress women or other men.

In my opinion, drinking alcohol, even a lot of it can be cultural. It may be cultural because of rampant depression; it may be cultural because of some rite of passage into manhood; it may be cultural because of water problems…a university lecturer being so drunk you can smell the alcohol standing a few meters away from him, cultural? Nope, that is a problem! At a minimum, it is a problem in a culture that is supposedly relational. Thinking it's no big deal for a university lecturer not being able to fulfill his duties because he is drunk is a major problem! The consumption of alcohol is no longer a unique cultural trait like Father Christmas; it is becoming a societal problem.

We had to become Vietnamese, I did not grow my pinky nails; neither did I find a mistress nor start drinking alcohol. Sue did not start cooking our meals with what seems like gallons of vegetable oil. Instead, we became relational.

Change #4. This change happened out of necessity, back in September 2006. I had 101 students, mostly girls who all looked identical and many of whom had the exact same names, or so I thought. "I know my sheep and my sheep know me (John 10:14 NIV, emphasis mine); I have called you by name, you are mine (Isaiah 43:1 NKJV, emphasis mine)." We took pictures of each student who had written her or his name above where their head would be, the pictures and names were put on 3X5 cards and used each day of class to learn names and faces and to think about each student before each class day. Soon, names and faces were known. We extended the idea to English language teachers and administrative staff members and School administrators too. Then, local townspeople were included. We became relational.

Sue and I weren't belligerent or wild but, we held hands and went to the market together. We used our typical Baby and Sweetheart and I love you language, as usual, whenever we went out and during phone conversations between each other.

We greeted people in town by name. We spoke holiday greetings in Vietnamese. We called every person we had any interaction with by their given name as much as possible. Frankly, we demonstrated what the culture claimed the people of the culture were, but for any number of reasons, had abandoned a long while ago.

<u>Change #5</u>. We no longer put our emphasis on "soul winning" (much to the dismay of some). Rather than attempt what would probably become a rather lengthy diatribe that might sound theological, let's point to two verses, "if I am lifted up, will draw all people to myself (John 12:32 NIV, bracket mine)," and, "whatever you do, do it all for the glory of God (1 Corinthians 10:31, NIV)." I call this His role, my (our) role. Someone has said that if we, God's people, make what is important to Him our priority, He will make what is important to us, His priority. NOT that soul winning isn't important, it is very important; however, the care of His creation is also important. Caring for some of His Vietnamese creation is important to Him too! So, we began doing everything we do, shopping, teaching, relating, everything in such a way as to bring glory to the Father! He has been drawing people and He will continue to draw people unto Himself! We are known as Christian people. We don't hide anything; we don't flaunt anything either.

Currently, we are actively involved in discipleship with some new, likeminded people. We meet regularly and pray together, eat together and study together. Sometimes we celebrate the Lords supper together. One decided, for Christ, almost three years ago, another much more recently. Still another has become aware of Hope and enjoys knowing Him!

Many more expectations are on the way out the window! A few are staying! We expect His word to produce fruit; fruit that will remain. We expect He will continue to draw people because His name continues to be used as the reason for what we do and the way we do it.

Think it over

1. What expectations do you have?

2. What expectations of yours go unmet continually or much of the time?

3. Perhaps it is time for completing the two tasks: List all of the expectations you have for _____; now, draw a line through every one of the expectations that you cannot personally guarantee the outcome of.

4. How many are left?

5. What will it take to get rid of those that you have drawn a line through?

6. What changes ought to be made after discarding those old expectations?

Chapter 10

Playing Hurt

"In 1950, [Ted] Williams was playing in his eighth All-Star Game. In the first inning, Williams caught a line drive by Ralph Kiner, slamming into the Comiskey Park scoreboard and breaking his left arm. *Williams played the rest of the game*[3], (emphasis by the author)."

Ted Williams was a great hitter. Ralph Kiner related the incident and injury cited above while broadcasting a baseball game, sometime in the latter 20th century. Kiner stated that, when asked about coming out of the game, an All-Star game, which back then had no impact on anything, Williams responded that the fans had come to see him play and they deserved to see him play the whole game.

My first trip to Vietnam was supposed to be my last. It was supposed to be a way to get some data for research on post-traumatic stress disorder (PTSD). But, to keep things simple, it wasn't my last trip. It was the first of four trips I was to make with a Christian humanitarian group of predominately Vietnam veterans who were focused on reconciling relations between themselves and Christ, between themselves and their former enemies and between themselves and their past experiences during the war. The primary way all of this was accomplished was by veterans, and, increasingly, non-veterans conducting free medical clinics in remote areas of central Vietnam and by building medical clinics, most often in remote areas of central Vietnam. Then, they are giving those clinics to the local Vietnamese health providers for

---

[3] Downloaded from Wikipedia, November 5, 2016, https://en.wikipedia.org/wiki/Ted_Williams

their use. All of this was done for the Vietnamese and Vietnam at no cost.

In August 2006, we moved to northern Vietnam to serve as a 'volunteer university lecturer and my non-teaching spouse' for two years. Eventually, Sue made her first trip with Vet's With A Mission (VWAM) and continued to participate. I was able to go on a few teams when the dates did not interfere with my teaching schedule. Somewhere along the way, we got the idea that our school, the School of Foreign Languages, Thai Nguyen University, should provide advanced-level students as interpreters for VWAM. Nothing is simple, easy, or quick in Vietnam, least of all a new, never done before idea.

In the spring of 2015, two hand-picked upper-level students of English were recruited, permissions, clearances and finances were acquired and four people left for Da Nang to provide interpreters for a soon-to-arrive VWAM team of volunteers.

At the airport in Hanoi, just before the announcement to begin boarding our flight to Da Nang, I go to the "little boy's room" soon after boarding the plane. Remember, *nothing is simple, easy, or quick in Vietnam*. While exiting the restroom, my foot engages the lip of the floor at the exit/entrance, tripping and falling to my knees. But, I could not get up. My left leg did not work! Sue's cell phone is turned off in anticipation of boarding the plane. One of the students starts looking for me but, she doesn't know exactly where I went. I am now on my knees and there are other people around, making it impossible to see me. I still cannot get up.

The short version: eventually, I crawl up the stairs onto the aircraft and a flight attendant brings lots of ice for my knee that now looks like the Incredible Hulk. Somehow, we all get to Da Nang, to the hotel and get somewhat settled. I cannot walk but it IS a medical team, with a bunch of medical professionals! Thank GOD! Eventually, after we are back in the United States for our summer break, an orthopedic specialist breaks the news. The tendon in the left leg that connects the top part of my leg to the bottom part is "gone" and needs to be replaced. "How long does that take?" I ask. "One day surgery and at least nine months' recuperation and therapy," they tell me.

"Nope, can't do that, I need to be back in Vietnam on August 5th!" "Well, here's your choices, surgery or limping." I took limping. I asked for and received a four-pronged cane (the terrain where we live in Vietnam is a little uneven) and decided we'd go back. I'd teach the first term and then come back for surgery late December 2015 or early January 2016. BUT THEN...

We returned to where we live, LOTS of stairs. We had arranged for all my classes to be on the first floor. We practiced walking to each classroom to make sure I could actually do it without falling down. Everything went very well, even the steep climb up a knoll to one of my classrooms (after a few times practicing). The term began; I only fell twice. Once, I fell during a class, which was a little embarrassing but, what could I do. One other time I fell when missing a step exiting a restaurant. I had to learn to take everything a lot slower than I was used to or liked...and by the end of the term I was ready for floors 1-5!

Sometime during that first term, I decided that I would not return to get surgery.

There are many reasons for the decision. After several weeks seeking wisdom from Father, and 99.9% sure I was not going to have surgery, something happened.

Many times, after teaching, I often stop at the pond and ate an apple, drank some water and just relaxed after my classes were finished for the day. On this day, I was sitting and eating an apple and in my heart "talking" to Father: I had been led to several scripture passages that seemed to be pointing towards a "no surgery" decision. I had re-read Practicing the Presence and noticed several similarities in our experiences such as, he had a 'bum' leg and, he did not like working in a kitchen when he first did that; my left leg caused me to limp and, way-back-when, I did not especially like teaching English. And, there were many others, too many to list but enough to lean me ever closer to avoiding surgery. Then, there was this university student.

This young man was being assisted to his class by some classmates who wheeled him to the classroom building and carried him, and the wheelchair, up to the second floor to class. "How can I bail?" I asked. "How can I retreat to the comfort of great medical care because of this limp, when he goes through all of that, every day of his life, just to get to school?" I could not justify it in my heart. "When the going gets tough, the American English teacher gets going…back to the safety of the West."

I successfully climbed the stairs, one-at-a-time, to the FIFTH floor (just to make sure I could do it), and then contacted the Chair of the English Language Department to tell her that for the second term, it would be good if she would schedule me for more hours, on any floor. I did ask to group as many classes in a row and to consolidate my classes on as few days as possible, to avoid having to walk back home, and then have to return again later the same day. She made it happen and as of this writing, it is working very well!

Some people, quite a few people come, literally, out of the jungle or down from a mountain and travel several hundred kilometers to go to university. Parents do whatever they can to come up with the money necessary to get their child through university. Like many places, there are those who are not very serious about studying; however, most are very serious, hanging their hope for the future on their education.

As we represent the One who created each of them (and us) for some purpose, and Who sent His Son in order to reconcile them (and us) to Himself, we must remember He has promised to never forsake [them].

How could I give up on them just because I have to walk a lot more slowly than ever before? I decided to "play hurt."

Think it over

One of our sons was a pretty good wrestler in high school. His team's T-shirt logo read, "If it were easy, everyone would do it."

Somethings are easy and everyone can do those things. And, playing "hurt" is not in and of itself an indicator of greatness, maturity, being close to sainthood or any other form of greatness. Making the choice to keep going when every fiber and many other people are saying "quit" is difficult. Frankly, it is not a decision that ought to be made, as a result of, consulting with "flesh and blood."

It takes practice, too.

- How many things are a part of your daily life, weekly, monthly, or yearly life? Does the thought of not doing any one of those things cause anxiety?

List them, starting from the one that causes the least anxiety to the most.

- Without announcing it to anyone, *anyone*, stop doing that first thing; replacing it with something else is a great idea.

- Continue with that first item, and continue to the next...decide how quickly to start the next thing (try to avoid taking more than a month to add something) ...and continue in a cumulative way, until you get through to the last thing.

- What does this have to do with "playing hurt?" Comfort is a norm. We tend to gravitate toward it. Training ourselves to embrace, even welcome discomfort might be radical; it certainly is "different" in a culture that expects instantaneous everything and anything exactly the way we want it every time we get it!

- Playing "hurt" is not comfortable. Many of us expect a timeout, a "flag on the play," a replay review or something to compensate for the "hurt." Most of us, maybe ALL of us want to be comfortable.

- To serve whomever we are or ought to be serving in our sphere, wife/husband, children, brother(s)/sister(s), the beneficiaries of whatever service we are providing, we must be willing to do so when it is anything but comfortable or convenient!

Chapter 11

Fruit that Will Remain

"I appointed you to go and produce lasting fruit... (John 15:16, NLT)."

"A good tree produces good fruit; and, a bad tree produces bad fruit (Matthew 7: 17, NLT)."

"You can identify them by their fruit... (Matthew 7:16, NLT)."

"So, every tree that does not produce good fruit is chopped down and thrown into the fire (Matthew 7:19, NLT)."

I have never been fond of "notching guns." Well, that's an exaggeration; actually, it would be more accurate to write; I am no longer fond of "notching guns."

From the time, I first became an infantry soldier until sometime after Mardi Gras 1986, I was very much interested in "notching my guns," especially "my" "M2 .50 caliber machinegun HB." The stories could take volumes, possibly; some have morphed into "almost legend." Generals have landed helicopters to shake my hand after watching me shoot. Instructors at the U.S. Army Jumpmaster School asked me to disassemble and reassemble the weapon again, several times, because they could not believe anyone could do so as fast as they'd seen me disassemble and reassemble one. Fortunately, things like that are relegated to the "older I get the better I was" category of conversations. Those are told less frequently as details (and which of the claims to fame are exaggerations, i.e. lies) become a bit fuzzy.

At the top of this chapter four verses are quoted. Verses #2, #3 and #4 fueled my "Christianized version of gun of notching." I wanted to be "the best" ...accurately defined, I wanted to make sure I was

"Heaven bound," had my "ticket punched" and was one of the "chosen few." I aimed to make sure that there was no way the Lord could ever say, "Get away from me, I don't know you." I was determined to make myself the "tree that produces good fruit," the person most easily identifiable as a Christian, "identified by my fruit." I did not know for a long time that that verse was written to help identify fakes!

I first heard someone speak about the first verse, "fruit that will remain" in late 1985. It was a phrase that became part of one of the mantras that many genuine believers in Christ recite chorally, seemingly on cue. Many pseudo-believers recite similarly same mantras: "God is good" ..." All the time;" and, "All the time"... "God is good;" "What do we pray for?" "Open doors, Favor, Fruit that will remain and Support;" "They will know we are Christians...," "By our love." Hundreds, maybe thousands of us recite and repeat these or other phrases that we do not mean, at least not when we are reciting or repeating them. For me, it became very similar to being sure I had my various Army identifiers, NCOA card, my AUSA card, my challenge coin(s), the 3 General Orders, and similar things on my person or in my mind, ready for regurgitation upon command. In one word, being genuine gave way to being proud...that's right, PRIDE!

We're all flawed, all of us (people). We hate it, and many of us will do almost anything to keep from being caught or exposed as flawed. This makes as much sense as "screen doors on a submarine."

When we first came to Vietnam, I was sure I was "God's gift to the organization that sent us." I was certain that no one could possibly have an upper hand on me with respect to "missing work."

That false sense of security ended up being responsible for my becoming what Oswald Chambers referred to as "a spiritual prig." In plain English, the word "jerk" might be substituted. Thankfully, the Word is 100% true, including the parts about not forsaking me, always providing an exit, and everything working out for good for me (and anyone else) who loves God and is fulfilling His purpose.

Finally, after years of "I" increasing and "He" decreasing, things were reversed. Suddenly, scriptures like "apart from Me, you can do nothing, nada, zip, zilch" (my embellishment) became relevant in my heart. Verses like, "I hate pride and arrogance (Proverbs 8:13, NIV)," and "may HE (emphasis mine) give you the desire of your heart" (i.e. favor with God and man in Vietnam) "and make your plans succeed (Psalm 20:4, NIV)." Also, "commit to the Lord whatever you do, and your plans will succeed (Proverbs 16:3, NIV)." The Apostle Paul writes about running a race. One of my mentors was feeling pretty good about himself when he turned 50. The fellow was expecting to see the finish line almost any second. But, he said, "I could hear the Lord saying: "Boy, if you turn your head just a little, you can still hear the sound of the starting gun going off." This might be called a paradox. The fact is that chronologically, I am over 60; but, the truth is in many areas I am a "novice" or, at best, a journeyman.

The TRUTH IS, because I (both of us) yielded to the sovereignty of God, putting the Lord at "the center" of our lives, beginning with not denying Him when what seemed like a good possibility. He has honored His promises and we can see that we have found "favor with the Lord and with [people] (1Samuel 2:26, NIV)."

All of that was in preparation for what's coming next. Boiled down to one thing, the reason for "the fruit," any of it…is because I (we)

followed the Spirit. It really was and still is that basic. Of course, the implication for whoever includes: being sure of "hearing," correctly & accurately, and then "obeying."

FRUIT We do not expect to see cranberries harvested in Florida or Honduras or in Vietnam; if we did, it would be weird. Our fruit will likely be different than what's expected in North America.

The response I received from my reply to the question, "SO, where did this agapé come from; who invented it?" "Jesus Christ" produced these follow-up questions: "Who is he; what state was he born in?" Now over 15 years later, we get some pretty amazing responses.

Dear Sue & Bill

I was deeply saddened to hear the death of your father. We know that he is now with God in a better place with his suffering gone. God will never give us more than we can bear, & he is with you through every step in your life. My thoughts and prayers are with you.

A Colleague

Thank you for praying and blessing me. I am so happy.
Phương (a former student)

I WOULD LIKE TO THANK GOD!
HE helped us to do well today!
I love God!
A Student

God has a plan for us
:D:D:D:D:D:D:D

"Yeah, my first time inside a church".
a colleague attending a course abroad

Wish you a happy birthday with lots of wonderful things! You are always my inspirational teacher! You rock! Love the way you are!

Mr. Bill, I want to write to you in case that I may forget to tell you. I have had a lot of teachers during my life but you're the one who is always by my side and whom I believe most. You're the one with whom I want to share my pain but also the one I don't want to share my sadness because I'm afraid that you'll be worried about me. You're the one who I can cry whenever I think of because of all your kindness. I can feel the peace whenever I am with you and I can feel the kindness in your eyes! I'm so grateful for having you in my life! A former student, current colleague

When I was your student, I used to play truant to teach extra. You hated the laziness and unpunctuality, so I knew you didn't like me. When I graduated from university and became a teacher, it was you who helped me how to be a good teacher. You always support me and stimulate me whenever I feel bored with my work. No matter how busy you are, if I say I need your help you will make plans to help me. I can't remember how many times you have spent your time visiting my school and seeing my teaching. I can't also count how many times you have helped me with my lessons as well as my English programs. That you are always proud of me and give me good compliments encourages me a lot. You are one of the kindest people I have ever met. Today is Vietnamese teacher's day; I wish you good health and happiness.

One of the Trang's:

P/s: In addition to your passion, enthusiasm, and kindness, I admire your love to your wife as well.

Recently, we had a visit from a protégé. The story is pretty incredible.

During our year in the U.S. (June 2012 – August 2013) a Vietnamese girl, university age, sent me a "friend request" on Facebook. The last thing I needed was another girl sending me messages. This girl was not one of my students. I did not know her.

Not every woman or young adult girl is beautiful, meaning attractive physically, only most of them are. In a class with a large number of males there can be 3, possibly 4. There is no need for me making "friends" with any woman on Facebook who I do not know. I rarely accept "friend requests" from women I do know, unless they are one of my students and I know them by name. I denied every request THIS person made, which was happening about every two days.

Someone gave her my e-mail. The e-mail read: "Mr. Bill, you are a famous English professor in Vietnam. I am trying to master the language. I need your help. Please, accept my friend request." After talking it over with Sue, and when we agreed, I accepted the request.

We returned to Vietnam on August 1, 2013. Within three days, "Hạnh" was at the door of our one room place. Hạnh explained the importance of her mastering the language and I agreed to meet with her weekly. Then I added, "There's no way this is going to work unless the Lord is involved. If you don't mind, I'd like to pray with you and ask for His help;" she said yes.

"Hạnh" became a "C-creature" the next Easter Sunday when we visited a local Fellowship to celebrate the Resurrection! We've been meeting together, Hạnh, Sue and me, several times a week ever since.

For many who have received Christ, life provides more than one rough patch. In the Book, we can read of the trials, tribulation, and persecution to be expected. It is often difficult to distinguish between "trials," "tribulation," and "persecution." I define them as: hassles or grief, opposition from the enemy of the Cross and bad things that happen, specifically because I am identified as a believer and follower of Christ. Pinpointing the source of the first two is more difficult than the third. In many experiences, hassles and grief are caused by my own stupidity, laziness, "flesh," and so on. Distinguishing those from opposition from "principalities and powers unseen" can be difficult. It can also waste time. It is true that the more "on-fire" a person is for the Lord, the more likely he or she is to experience either opposition and/or persecution.

After graduating, Hạnh decided to go into business. Opening a language learning center in the town where she attended university, instead of returning to her hometown was wonderful, adventurous, and *not* something many university graduates would decide to do, particularly a single Vietnamese woman.

Hạnh sought the Lord, we did too. She believes her plan is "OK with the Lord" and that "He will take care of me, He always does."

Hạnh had also previously committed to helping lead an interpreter project in early April 2017.

Soon fear began to creep in and raise doubts about being able to honor the previous commitment. Quickly, talk of "I might not be able to…" began to pop up. We (Sue and I) gave Hạnh space to seek the direction of the Lord. We offered a couple of scenarios; including the possibility that it may be that she should not be a part of the project. Mainly, we prescribed praying and seeking His wisdom and direction.

Without any interference from us, Hạnh prayed through and decided that she was doing both, establishing the learning center and helping to lead the interpreter project in April 2017. FRUIT!

Some fruit takes longer to grow than others

Bính was one of our first students in 2006. Bính was present when I was asked and answered the question "Why did you and your wife come to Vietnam." Bính has known about our relationship to Christ almost from the beginning. Frankly, since 2006, it has never specifically come up in any personal conversation.

In 2015, Sue and I became the first foreigners ever to be given residency cards from the government of Vietnam, who are not members of a Non-Government Organization (an NGO). We had not requested them; we were not expecting them; and, it would be accurate to say, nothing like that had ever been considered possible.

Bính was the Director of the Office of International Relations from spring 2014 – February 2017. In May 2016, Bính came to our apartment on business and after exchanging pleasantries said, "Mr. Bill, you are the first person ever to be given a resident card and not be part of an NGO. God had to be involved for this to happen; it has never happened before!"

To me, this statement is right up there with statements made by King Nebuchadnezzar and the Pharaoh of Egypt in Old Testament history.

Frankly, we have decided to give the Lord space in determining the steps involved in moving people we serve from no God to knowing God personally.

Think it over

Everyone enjoys being successful. There is nothing inherently "wrong" with wanting to do a good job, accomplishing goals or enjoying success from efforts made.

In Exodus, God wrote, "You shall have no other gods before Me (NASB)." Jesus explains that loving God with "everything you've got" is one of the two most important commandments given by God and that the two together "sum up" or "fulfill" all the other commandments of God (see Matthew 22:37-40, NIV)!

Often, we think about false gods as Buddha, or one of the hundreds of Hindu gods, or Allah and, they are. But, there are many others, too. Sometimes we can miss some or all of them.

When I can recite statistics about all the World Series championships of the New York Yankees more readily than all 66 books of the Bible, there may be a false god before Him. When I am basing my conduct, behavior, habits and so forth primarily on what makes my spouse happy, on what makes me happy, on what my boss expects or in comparison to what anyone else thinks or is doing rather than on what pleases my Father in Heaven, there may be a false god before Him.

A huge obstacle to enjoying and producing "fruit that will remain" is having a "false god." Sometimes I've been guilty of putting myself before the One True God with me increasing and Him decreasing, rather than the other way around. This "god" can go by the name "pride" or "tradition" or "narrowmindedness." I had to reorder my life. I did that by placing Christ at the center of my life rather than adding Christ as just another part of my life. I had to make a conscious choice to do everything that I do for the glory of God. I had to develop the habit of seeking, asking, crediting, thanking, praising the Lord first. It took a while, but eventually the habit stuck (most of the time).

And now consider…

1. How do you feel about "notching your guns?"

2. Is it important that you get "credit" for any or all the accomplishments you experience?

3. How strong is the pull-of-pride in your life, spirit, heart, and mind?

4. Do you give token credit to God by prefacing "I did phrases" with statements such as: "All glory to God, of course, but *I*...?"

5. How do you measure "fruit," i.e. things that have occurred directly or in directly of Jesus (but in a straight line) because of some service you have done in the Name and for His glory?

6. What is the appropriate balance between personal highlight reels versus genuine humility?

7. What "fruit" is there from your being a God-pleasing spouse; a God-pleasing daughter or son; a God-pleasing parent; a God-pleasing employee; a God-pleasing student?

Chapter 12

Imagination or Vision

"It was just my imagination…running away with me."

"Write the vision, make it [easy to understand] so that [you can] run with it (NIV)."

I am sometimes asked "Why did you choose Vietnam" or "How did you know the Lord was leading you to Vietnam?"

Many people imagine things, maybe all of us do. Without getting into a debate about imagination versus dreams versus vision versus idea, versus audible or inaudible, and all other possible and potential controversies, here we identify "imagination" as an idea I conjure up on my own. "Vision" is something we "get" specifically from the Lord.

Lots of us imagine, fewer have God-sent, God-inspired, God-initiated visions. I have mistaken the common (my imagination) as vision (a "God-thing") many times.

When I first got joined the U.S. Army, I imagined the girls would swoon over me in my uniform; they didn't. When I got my first tattoo, I imagined myself with huge, rock hard biceps; it did not happen. When I first accepted Christ and became an infantry soldier, a Non-commissioned Officer, I imagined that I could "order" subordinates to accept Christ; it never worked out that way (thank God!).

Sometime after my first few witnessing trips to New Orleans, I imagined a "state miniature" of the organization that I had become involved with in going to New Orleans, including a smaller version of the bus, and automatically connecting with every other "state miniature" for "the Cause;" this one actually got off to a sputtering start that had at least a few good things happen as a result; but, that too was my idea not His.

The first vision I ever had, which actually came from the Lord was heard, not seen. It was a vision I heard after coming out of a coma like thing, and after realizing that I had no idea about how to have a real relationship with the Lord. I had been "saved" for nearly 10 years. I had no idea how the Lord communicated with me. I had come to the conclusion that "I must be doing OK, since I had never heard from the Lord otherwise." Basically, I committed to following the Lord "110%." I assumed He would teach me how He communicated with me. The result of that encounter is still on-going. Then, in early 1986, I had a vision of becoming a husband that pleases God first, even before pleasing my wife. Another on-going experience.

Most of the time, the Lord communicates with me through His written word.

It began with reading the Proverb for the day; the Book of Proverbs has 31 chapters, one for each day of a month. My habit of hearing from the Lord through His word began with reading the proverbs. Somewhere along the line, both my wife and I began to read the Bible through each year.

Many people whistle. My Dad whistled. My Dad whistled without pursing his lips or putting fingers near his mouth; I have no idea how he did it. I've never been able to imitate his whistle. If my Dad whistled, I could hear it and knew he was whistling to get my attention. I don't know how; I just knew that I could; even now, decades since I last heard that whistle, I can still "hear" it.

I cannot explain how God communicates to me through the Word; I just know that when He does. I "hear" Him. Perhaps it comes from knowing Him so well after all these years. I know that I recognize "His voice" when I "hear" it.

It bears repeating, so again…

My wife Sue and I had finished our time at a home for first-time single mothers. We had served there for three years. When we arrived in our house in Missouri, Sue asked, "So, what are we going to do next (which is code for, "Where are we going to get money from now")?" We agreed to pray and seek God's will and pleasure for 30 days.

We prayed.

The word and the place, Vietnam, continually popped into my thoughts. I dismissed it as a distraction. Frankly, I do not recall any other idea, thing or possibility being "in the hopper." I do remember my first, second and even third reaction to the idea that the Lord might be leading me, and us, to Vietnam.

NO!

We were going to Honduras...I had been going to Honduras regularly for 10 years. I could sing several praise songs and choruses in Spanish. I had dreams of us being "missionaries" sitting on a beach sipping non-alcoholic piña coladas...I did not *want* to go to Vietnam, *wah, wah, wah*!

But then, I recalled the dream of another person; Jesus, the Rock, falling onto Honduras and the ripples radiating from the splash He made. The ripples represented the Good News and how the Story would emanate around the world from Honduras, what this person calls "the land of the Anointing." As I was praying I eventually could "see" in my mind's eye, one of the ripples touching Vietnam. *I was convinced.*

Then, I noticed that Vietnam and Honduras are on the same parallel geographically in different hemispheres. Then, I met a "missionary" who had good and convincing evidence that the first occupants of North America came from what is called Ho Chi Minh City and Seoul today. I was intrigued and I was hooked.

Sue, my wife, was not convinced.

Honestly, flashes of the old "I'm the king of my castle" became gigantic. The Spirit prevailed and after just over a year of praying and seeking "open doors" and every single item on a long list of "must happen in order for this to happen" being fulfilled, we BOTH were on an airplane heading to Vietnam.

As I have stated, our agreement was two whole years! How are we ever going to survive, and other questions popped into our minds. Now, over 10 years later, we can testify that this was and still is where we needed and need to be!

It was and is important for me, both my wife and me, to have a scriptural basis for determining God's desire, plan, will and specific function He has for us. Of course, lots of people can read almost anything into scripture that they want to justify all sorts of ungodly things, such as discrimination against people who have dark skin, slaughter of Muslims, and husbands lording it over their wives are just three examples.

I have no desire to write annotated bibliography of references regarding our decision. I have no need or desire to fully explain every single situation and its application to our decision to "hear" or "see," accept, and carry out what we are sure is God's plan and purpose for us. Instead, here is a list and description of the scriptures we use to confirm this as our life's purpose.

We acknowledge that we have been "transformed by the renewing of [our] minds [thinking] (Romans 12:2, NIV);" and, that "we have the mind of Christ (1Corinthians 2:16, NIV)." Thus, I no longer can consider Vietnam or Vietnamese people, even those few my age and older, as an enemy. I also have to acknowledge that when I read that God "desires ALL PEOPLE EVERYWHERE" it opens up the Kingdom to Vietnamese people too.

Forgive my partiality when I refer to His words, "Go teach." I know it is a little out of context but ultimately, what we are teaching is included in all He has told us. I remember reading on a sign, in Honduras, "Whom shall I send; and who will go for us?"

It was not the first time I'd read it but, given that at the time I was standing in Honduras and Vietnam was "on my mind," it "clicked," and I responded with "I'll go!"

"Let your light shine before [people] (Matthew 5:16, NIV);" "Ask of Me and I will make the [nation, Vietnam] your inheritance (Psalm 2:8, NIV)." We did, we have and now, we are "almost Vietnamese." "The earth is the Lord's and everything [everyone] in it (NIV);" "He rules over the nations (NIV);" "For God is King of ALL the earth;" and, I confessed, "You, Lord, are the Most High OVER ALL THE EARTH [including Vietnam] (NIV, emphasis added)."

He has the authority to send us here if He wants to.

In Psalm 37 we read, "…and He will give you the desires of your heart." I used that verse as grounds for getting whatever I wanted or desired. But then, my understanding changed to He (God, the Lord) will give me (place) godly desires into my heart. Doubters, anyone relying on flesh, will say that I mean that God manipulated my heart to get what He wants rather than what I want. No, that's not true. It is more like acquiring an appreciation for a different style of music or watching the kind of movies my wife likes to watch and enjoying it.

In the Book of Nehemiah, I read how Eliashib and his fellow priests rebuilt one section of the wall; the men of Jericho, the next section, Zaccur next to him, the Fish Gate by the sons of Hassenaah, and so on. Considering the application of the concept of rebuilding the wall around Jerusalem in the context of rebuilding/repairing a breach in the "wall" of the Kingdom of God on the earth, specifically "the section" known as Vietnam, our purpose or function is to "repair," i.e. eliminate the breach, in the wall of His creation and "stand in the gap" for His people who the world calls Vietnam and Vietnamese.

Like so many others from my generation who were soldiers, Vietnam and Vietnamese people were "the enemy!" Why would I want to help them? Like Peter, I was shown that I should not call anyone impure or unclean or, in this context, ineligible to be blessed through two people who are madly in love and 100% committed to their Lord, Jesus Christ. Similarly, and as he writes, "I realized how true it is that God does not show favoritism but accepts [people] from every nation who fear Him and do what is right (Acts 10:34,35, NIV)." A dear friend, a veteran from the war in Vietnam, can often be heard to say, "the past is the past at last."

I was an infantry soldier and I so walked a lot. Paul the Apostle walked a lot too, a lot more than I did, I think. I developed an appreciation, even a like by identification, with Paul because he was "the Lord's infantryman" and because he was a man who could "tell it like it is," like I often do. This is a stretch, I admit it, but...here's my calculation:

I delight myself in the Lord + He gives me the desires of my heart + Paul ...having been kept by the Spirit from...the province of Asia (emphasis added) + "greater works than these" + for such a time as this= "I get to do what Paul was not allowed to do. In fact, maybe he was kept from going into Asia just so we could go and make a difference in many lives there!"

My last scripture verse is found in the Gospel, according to John. In his twelfth chapter, we are commissioned to lift up Jesus Christ and assured that, when we do lift Him up, e.g. when given an opportunity to explain why we ever came and are living in Vietnam, He will draw people to Himself (John 12:32 NIV).

People often ask questions like "How did you know that God wanted you to go to Vietnam?"

Our answers are simple AND complicated. Basically, we know Him well and everything we have read, seen, experienced, and are currently experiencing pointed and points to us being exactly where we have been, are, and will be for the foreseeable future.

Think it over

1. What is God's purpose for your life?

2. What were you created for?

3. What skill set do you possess?

4. What do you like doing the most?

5. Do you limit what God can use you for by considering an area or skill or "favorite thing" in your life as being unusable?

6. What about raising children, being a great Dad or Mom?

7. What about an ability to hit a baseball a very long way, every time or almost every time you swing at one?

8. What about your passion, what really gets you going; is it transferable to the Kingdom?

9. Is there anything keeping you from pursuing the purpose for which you were created?

10. What steps are you willing to make to eliminate the "competition?"

11. What would it "sound like," "read like" or "look like" for you to receive God's vision for your life?

Conclusion

Our lives are unique, but not that special really. Our adventure in Vietnam continues for as long as God allows. It is our joy to share with you, the reader, a bit of our incredible story...again, unique but all of God's people who are truly yielded to Him can accomplish much...for us Vietnamese fruit...fruit that remains... for you...God knows...ask Him!

Epilogue

Still in the neighborhood

February 2017

We both want to be in Vietnam. Currently, we are asking the School of Foreign Languages, Thai Nguyen University to extend or renew our contract and residential status until June 2025; we would both be going on 70.

There is only one thing that I have done that I stated at the beginning I wanted to do for the rest of my life that I actually will do for the rest of my life, be Sue McDonald's husband.

As long as I am physically and mentally able to function as a lecturer and teacher at the university level here in Vietnam, and be effective and affective (in the lives of colleagues, neighbors and most of all students), I want to be here.

In a few days, we will have lunch with one "C-creature," a former student, and supper with another, after she spends a few hours with a congregation celebrating and worshipping the Lord!

A few hours before writing this last part, I was in a class of third-year students, many of whom I taught as freshmen and sophomores, who have embraced the possibility that they have a legitimate possibility of experiencing levels of success, proficiency, happiness, and fulfillment that very few ever would have considered 2 and ½ years ago. Also, a short while ago, in just a few moments, my wife Sue explained how to make pumpkin soup, simply and from "scratch" to a Vietnamese woman and the woman burst into compliments and gratitude for enlightening her life!

We're on a roll; and, we're experiencing "all things working together for good."

It is my hope that visions will be sought and realized, activated, materialized, and fulfilled by some who read this adventure.

Nó không nhận được bất kỳ tốt hơn thế này [it doesn't get any better than this].

Cảm ơn bạn, Chúa Giêsu!

Bill McDonald